Key to the thumb

Also by Ron Moody

THE DEVIL YOU DON'T

VERY VERY SLIGHTLY IMPERFECT

OFF the CUFF

The Do-it-yourself, Anywhere, Anytime Instant Bookspeech

RON MOODY

Illustrations by the Author

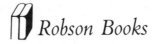

Robson Books

First published in Great Britain in 1987 by Robson Books Ltd, Bolsover House, 5-6 Clipstone Street, London W1P 7EB.

British Library Cataloguing in Publication Data

Moody, Ron
   Off the cuff,
   1. Public speaking
   I. Title
   808.5′1   PN4121

ISBN 0-86051-459-5

Printed in Great Britain by A. Wheaton & Co Ltd, Exeter, Devon.
Bound by Dorstel Press Ltd, Harlow, Essex.

Contents

Foreword

There is no determinate time in life to make your mark. It's never too early, never too late. Mozart wrote his first piano sonatas at the age of seven and published them in Paris, a year later, to keep himself in lollipops. Wibrecht, the King of Prussia's tuba virtuoso, developed his exemplary embouchure at the incredible age of three months – much to the anguish of his mother who was feeding him at the time.

Not having their patience, I made my first successful speech at the age of fifty-one. By 'successful' I mean there was some laughter, faces, in general, were turned towards me, and four people spoke to me on the way out. Three were looking for the exit, but there was praise too. Before that time, my attempts to speak in public were as cheerful as a sing-along in a leper colony. I didn't do much better in private.

So, where did I go right? And where can you, if you haven't already? Because you can! Unless you can't. Don't misunderstand me. You may not have the genes to write a sonata, you may lack the chromosomes to develop your embouchure and stun your girl (or boy) friend. You may simply not have been born with the DNA to take six wickets, top the pops, hang a glide or mount Everest. But you *can* make a successful speech! If, that is, you are marginally intelligent, moderately articulate and mildly determined. You won't make it if you are simple-minded, slack-jawed and wet. Only in parliament. Where the ability to speak at all is a bonus.

So, what's the trick? Well, let's say it's more of a three-card trick, based on the proposition that the punters are dying to be taken in, you can deliver the spiel, and you play your cards right, viz:

    (1) DICTION (BEING HEARD)
    (2) DELIVERY (BEING FELT)
    (3) DISCOURSE (BEING UNDERSTOOD)

(1) *Diction*

If you haven't got this, you'll have to buy another book (by Greta Colson or Cecily Berry) or take a course at the City Lit. Failing that, try rehearsing with a tape recorder. If *you* can't hear what *you* are saying when you play it back, first check the battery, then do it again. Only this time, mark the script, underlining key words to be accented, and marking, particularly, final consonants, final 'T's, 'D's, 'M's, and 'N's, and, if you're a Cockney, middle 'L's. Then exaggerate their pronunciation – OVER-ARTICULATE! – otherwise, instead of 'oNe piNT oF skiMMeD miLK anD a carTON oF creaM', you'll get: WUM PI NA SKI MIOOG ANA CARNA CREE.

(2) *Delivery*

In theatrical parlance, projection, or if you prefer, impact, contact, holding the audience, dominating the audience, to wit, the element of performance! (Any two will do. Or three.) If you have no methods of your own, these come free with the book:

(a) Don't *learn* the lines, *read* them from the carefully prepared script and don't deviate from the text. That way, all your energy goes into the delivery and is not wasted, fumbling for words or ideas or thinking of places you'd much rather be. On the other hand, you can sell a joke better if you know it by heart.

(b) Don't think about reading the lines as *yourself* but adopt a *persona*, act a part. I deliver the lines like a very important person (that's really acting!) who turns out to be a grandiloquent klutz. If you don't like that idea, do it another way. Be a dry but genial pedant (Harold MacMillan), a giggling clown (Harry Secombe), a dead-pan pessimist (Clement Freud), or a warm and witty raconteur (Peter Ustinov), and only if you're really stuck be yourself. Which, oddly enough, is how you'll come over, anyway.

(c) Whatever you do, take a point of view, and *sell* it. And it *will work*! Most times.

(3) *Discourse*

Here is where this book comes into its own, goes beyond the tenuous presumptions of giving advice about speech making, or anything else for that matter. It is not a manual with rules and regulations to observe and which nobody ever reads beyond the index. That's too much like hard work.

No, in this case, like instant coffee, the book *is* the speech. The book *is* a carefully structured statement with

7

a beginning, a middle and an end (with variations on each), and it can last three minutes, thirty minutes, or far too long, depending which route you select through the sections outlined in the index, and which apposite jokes, quotations and toasts you decide to bring in from the appendices. Or put in yourself. It's your speech.

One more thing. I presume that you agree the speech should be funny. And this Bookspeech is generally designed to make people laugh because it comes after lunch or dinner, and on a full stomach it's better to help the digestion than induce sleep. To this end, it has been tested on every kind of audience, from a croupiers' convention to a Lord Mayor's banquet, and it has had every kind of reception, from a polite shunt in its early days to a standing ovation by the time it was broken in.

So, if you read the Bookspeech carefully, study its potential, and use it well, you will be able to hold your own at any wedding, fund-raising, tribute, company or social gathering or more, at long or short notice or less. Above all, apply your own ingenuity in choosing your route through the book, so that it becomes your point of view. Henry Irving said: 'If you do not pass a character through your own mind, it can never be sincere.'

So good eating, good drinking, good speaking and good luck – you great fat drunken demagogue!

RON MOODY
1987

How the
Bookspeech
works

Master plan

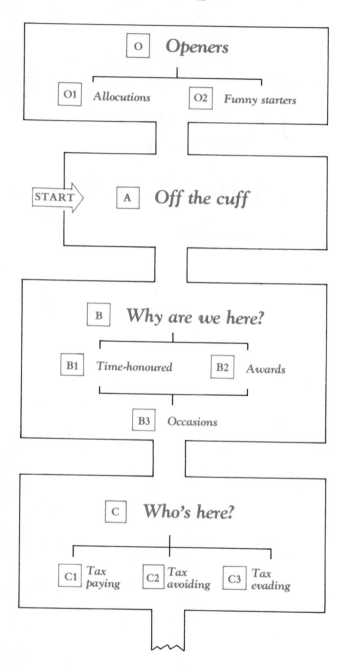

O **Openers**

O1 *Allocutions*   O2 *Funny starters*

START A **Off the cuff**

B **Why are we here?**

B1 *Time-honoured*   B2 *Awards*

B3 *Occasions*

C **Who's here?**

C1 *Tax paying*   C2 *Tax avoiding*   C3 *Tax evading*

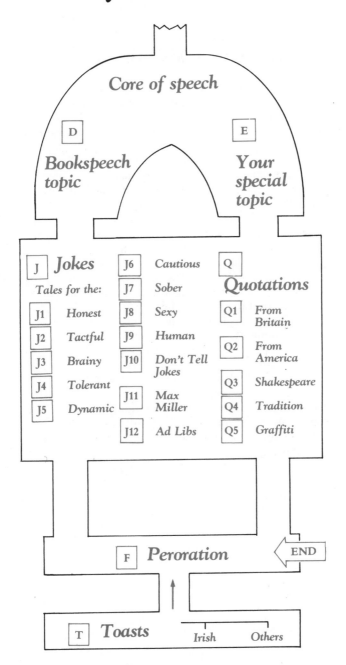

Selecting

Example one: a six-minute speech

For most after-dinner speeches, where, for example, you are making an appeal for charity, or paying tribute to a trusted friend, or even to your employer, landlord or probation officer, six minutes is more than enough to cook your goose. Especially if there are other speakers unwise enough to share your platform. As somebody once said: 'Span of concentration decrease in inverse proportion to ban on intoxication', and it wasn't Confucius.

Here is a typical six-minute format which you can trace through the book. Imagine, for starters, that we have an *individual* guest of honour, not a company or charity, or any similar *group*.

Your name is Mr Browne and your wife is Bertha Browne, and you are giving a small lunch at the Hilton Hotel for Bertha's 50th birthday. Since you should (by now) have personal knowledge of dear Bertha, you will take in route $\boxed{E}$, in which section you write and research your special topic, the biographical backdrop to Bertha Browne.

Or you may decide to take the route to $\boxed{D}$, the generalised, ready-written centrepiece, either because you haven't time to do your own thing or because you don't want to let any old cats out of any old bags.

Either way, you can draw on jokes and quotations in the appendix.

NOTE: fill in names and other specific details in the spaces provided, with a pencil, so that you can rub it out and use the Bookspeech more than once. Come to think of it, do it in ink, and buy another Bookspeech.

a route

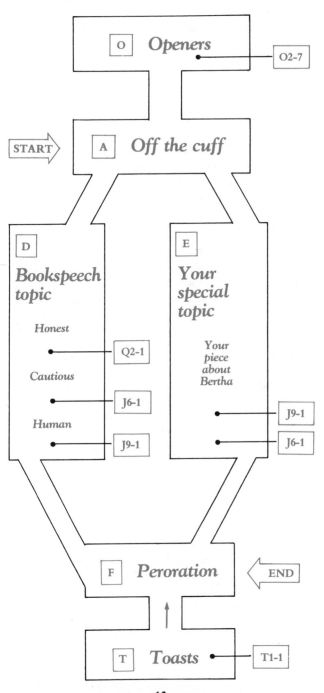

Example two: a fifteen-minute special

If they ask you to speak for fifteen minutes or more, they are really asking you to entertain them, and that's a different ball-game, a professional arena. Stand-up comics can rattle off an hour of jokes of various hues, mostly blues, without fear of innovation; sporting celebrities can dish up the dirt on clubs and managers without fear of litigation; and practised raconteurs can do their witty bit without fear of actually saying anything.

These professionals have one basic, tested speech, usually of a high quality, which they adapt, minimally, for each occasion. You might say this isn't, strictly speaking, too much concerned with the purpose of the gathering, until you see them tearing up a gaggle of half-cut, giggling women at their annual, festive lunch, or a mob of whole-cut, sniggering stock-brokers at their annual festive dinner. Subtlety and wit are gone with the festive wind. In fact, the festive wind is the only thing they *will* go with. Unless you are one of them. And come up with all the in-jokes.

The problem arises when you are *not* one of them, but you have to *relate* to them. That's why, in all formats of this master Bookspeech, there are lots of dotted lines to *pencil* in personal facts, names, ranks and reputations, and hints on how to switch the jokes to suit the occasions rather than just telling them. Which means you have to do your homework and find out who's who and what's what.

Well then. Here is a typical fifteen-minute format which you can trace through the book, imagining, this time, that you do *not* have an *individual* guest of honour, but have been asked to speak at the annual awards dinner of the Nearham Rotary Club. Assuming you have no personal knowledge of the group, you can route through section $\boxed{D}$, the generalised centrepiece. If, however, you are expected to present the awards, or wish to drag in your own little party piece, take the $\boxed{E}$ route.

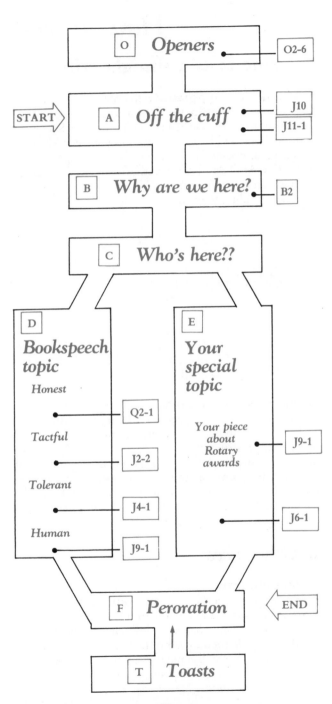

15

How to read

1 Using it as a straight crib

First variation: 'off-guard' delivery

This is the normal use of the Bookspeech: as a gag, where you claim that you have been caught off guard, happen to have the book and hope you can find your way through it. Then, although you deliver the main speech (IN BLACK CAPITALS) with authority, you also mutter the instructions (IN RED CAPITALS) as if you are genuinely finding your way.

For example:

'IF STILL NOT SURE OF THIS MOB, GO TO [C] .'

'IF THEY LAUGH AT *THIS*, GO TO SEALED SECTION AT THE BACK.'

OR

'DON'T MIND IF THEY WALK OUT… IT'S WHEN THEY START COMING TOWARDS YOU, YOU SHOULD WORRY!'

Second variation: natural delivery

You can read the main speech (IN BLACK CAPITALS) as if it is a continuous and natural narrative, ignoring all procedural instructions (IN RED CAPITALS). No mention is made of the Bookspeech as the source of material; it appears merely as a substitute for cards or typed sheets, and humour will come only from the content and context of the speech and any topical quips or comments you may have inserted.

2 Other uses

Formal blueprint

If you use Bookspeech and your office junior uses the Bookspeech and your whole firm uses the Bookspeech, and, it should only happen, thousands of people buy the Bookspeech, then sooner or later you'll go to a dinner and every speaker will stand up and make a Bookspeech. And even if this doesn't happen, *you* may need to address the same group twice. Never fear!

the Bookspeech

You can then use this book as a formal blueprint, a strategic pattern, that is, as a basis for a *new*, independently written speech, rather as you would switch an old joke to a new context. (SEE J9-1 .) Well, it's better than ploughing through a speechmaker's manual – it starts you off! It's not theorising, it's *doing*! *Do it!*

Source book

At the very least, it can be a source book (which you can continue to build up with your own collected jokes, quotations and bon mots) for material in your very own master speech.

Great comedians like Max Miller and Milton Berle had vast funds of jokes and gags stored in their cerebral encyclopaedias, and as they gauged their audience they would switch to an appropriate routine. Well, your source book is a pocket encyclopaedia, a nucleus.

The ethnic slant

I donated most of my formative years (and thereby gained most of my experience as comedian, speechmaker and entertainer) to weddings, barmitzvahs, and the obsession with charitable activity that simmers in the soul of every Semite.

I have included some of these here, as well as jokes and quotations from other religions and cultures, to encourage you to switch in your own ethnic nuances.

The shared secrets and sense of community engendered by this approach will make a powerful impact on your audience. It is, after all, merely a variant on the in-joke, the cultural frame of reference of any social group that defines its identity. That makes it a 'family'. And when you speak to your 'family', whether it be a family of policemen, tourists on the QE2, nurses, doctors, show people, show jumpers or even tax collectors, the mere mention of the 'family' buffoon or any other common target for ridicule, will, as in intimate revue, bring the roof down.

Do your own thing

So that's it. The Bookspeech. A starting point, a reality, a speech for all seasons, but most of all, a springboard to your own creative fulfilment.

Maimonides said that the highest degree of charity is 'when he, who by a gift or loan or finding employment, helps a fellow man to support *himself*' (Q4-1).

Well this book is a gift of ideas, a loan of techniques (and, as for finding employment, I don't even want ten percent, just buy the book) all these things to help you *outgrow* the Bookspeech and make your *own* commentaries on the world and its people.

Mazel tov... I mean, Bonne chance... Glück... Buona fortuna... Good luck!

The
Bookspeech

NOTE: *a brief selection of correct allocutions and humorous openers will be found in appendix* $\boxed{O}$.
On the left hand pages throughout this book I have given examples of how a speech would be made to the Nearham Rotary Club at its annual awards dinner at the Holiday Inn. You can try it with Bertha Browne's birthday lunch at the Hilton.

At M15 trial...

Mr Chairman, ladies and gentlemen, and members of the Nearham Rotary Club...

The Holiday Inn coffee shop...

Off the cuff

Improvisations for all occasions

WHEN ASKED TO MAKE UNEXPECTED SPEECH TO AUDIENCE THAT LOOKS MORE LIKE *JURY*, **(topical line here)** ....
....
....

SMILE BOLDLY **(smile boldly)** AND SAY:
....
....
....
....
....

WELCOME TO ....
....
....
....
....

AND NOW WILL YOU PLEASE TALK AMONGST YOURSELVES FOR A MOMENT
....

AND GO TO $\Longrightarrow$

FOR SHORT SPEECH TO: D
          OR   E

FOR EXTENDED SPEECH TO: J10
          OR   B
          OR   C

NOTE: *in this section we make our ties with the hosts or guests by touching on the purpose of the gathering before going on to the core of the speech. You may use either of the two options printed here, or write in your own.*

B1 *The first option humorously involves a known individual, be he chairman, Lord Mayor, the guest of honour, or your wife.*

Dinners

The Rotarians

Your chairman, Mr John Smith, a gentleman

'His/her/your/their – er? – HER ... HIS! ...

Why are we here?

PURPOSE OF THE GATHERING.

B1 *Time-honoured event*

HERE WE ARE AGAIN AT YET ANOTHER OF THOSE TIME-HONOURED

....

THAT HAVE BECOME A TIME-HONOURED TRADITION OF ....

....

AND IN THE PRESENCE OF ....
(rank and name) ....

....

....

WHO TIME HAS RENDERED HONOURED – ER – *AGELESS*, AND AGE HAS RENDERED HARMLESS – ER — *TIMELESS* – ER – (mutter quickly) *TIME* HAS RENDERED *AGELESS* AND *AGE* HAS RENDERED *TIMELESS*.
(Beam with relief)
WHAT A DISTINGUISHED OCCASION! AN OCCASION SO DISTINGUISHED I CAN'T *WAIT* TO HEAR WHAT I'M GOING TO SAY TO YOU FOR THE NEXT 45 MINUTES!

BECAUSE IT IS A CELEBRATION OF

....

GO TO ⟹ B3

23

NOTE: *this option is another kind of symbiosis, setting up and sending up the ludicrous excess of awards wingdings that cast serious doubts on the sanity of the judges.*

There are also endless sprees that raise funds and pay tributes. None of them are too thick-skinned to endure a sliver of satire, as long as you tell them how wonderful they are in the peroration.

Awards

Award

Dinner

Dinners

Award

The Nearham Rotary Club's

TO MANY OF YOU, THIS GATHERING MAY APPEAR TO BE JUST ONE MORE IN THE *ENDLESS* STREAM OF ....
DINNERS AND LUNCHES AND BANQUETS AND BALLS, THAT HAVE NOW REACHED SUCH *ENORMOUS* PROPORTIONS THAT THERE MUST SOON BE A DINNER TO ....

....
THE PEOPLE WHO *ATTEND* ALL THE DINNERS... AND LUNCHES AND BANQUETS AND BALLS.

THE INNOCENT AMONGST YOU MAY ASK: 'WHEREFORE, THEN, IS THIS ....
DIFFERENT FROM ALL THE OTHER ....

....
IT IS DIFFERENT BECAUSE WE ARE NOT HERE TO ....

....
THE MOST BEAUTIFUL OR THE MOST SEXY OR THE MOST PROVOCATIVE... WE ARE NOT HERE TO *ENJOY* OURSELVES! NO, WE ARE HERE TO CELEBRATE ....

....
....

GO TO ⟶ B3

NOTE: *there is a lot of fun to be had, reading out the lists of possible occasions, especially those least appropriate to the gathering. Read out more than half a dozen before you find the one you want.*

For example, at a company dinner, read the left hand column first, at a wedding supper, read the right hand column first. And put in a few of your own.

Annual Public Spectacle, I beg your pardon, Annual AWARDS!

B3 *Stating the occasion*

⟹ SELECT OCCASION

INDIVIDUAL

BIRTH

BIRTHDAY

CIRCUMCISION
– *BRIS* – A SMALL
SURGICAL
PROCEDURE THAT
THE JEWS HAVE
TURNED INTO A
CATERED AFFAIR

BARMITZVAH

GO TO ⟹ Q4-4

21ST BIRTHDAY
(IF A WOMAN, THIS
WILL DO FOR ALL
AGES: IF A MAN,
TRY 39TH)

ENGAGEMENT

WEDDING

TRIBUTE

RETIREMENT

VALEDICTION

SOCIAL

CHARITY BASH

AUCTION

FUND-RAISING FLING

ANNUAL COMPANY
CAPER

TEA DANCE

PERENNIAL
POTATION

ANNUAL PUBLIC
SPECTACLE

ANNUAL AWARDS

PROFESSIONAL
PUB CRAWL

BATTALION
BLOW-OUT

NAVAL JAG

ANNUAL XMAS
CRACK-UP

GASTRONOMICAL
ORGY

IF STILL NOT SURE OF THIS MOB
GO TO ⟹ C

OR IF EVEN HALF OF THEM APPEAR TO BE
SMILING   GO TO ⟹ D or E

27

NOTE: *this is another optional preliminary gambit, which extends the speech before going to the core.*
The provocative instructions about the audience will relate your speech to them, even if you aren't a member.

NOTE: *if you are speaking to a Jewish audience, put this section third. Similarly, with any other ethnic group. You merely have to change the typical professions and initials and other shared secrets.*

NOTE: *if your host professionals come in here, make sure they are mentioned last...*

Rotary Club members

Who's here?

LOOK CAREFULLY AROUND THE ASSEMBLY.

ONE:

IF YOU ARE FACING A BUNCH OF CLEAN-LIMBED, HEALTHY, DECENT, UPRIGHT, SOBER,
TAX-PAYING
CITIZENS...

GO TO ⟹ BIBLE READINGS
(*OR* : look around, shake head and say:
'TWO')

TWO:

IF THEY ARE LAWYERS, ACCOUNTANTS, DOCTORS, SPECIALISTS, RAG TRADE, HAIR TRADE, JIA, WIZO, AND OTHER
TAX-AVOIDING
TEETOTALLERS...

GO TO ⟹ JEWISH JOKES, AND STAY THERE!

THREE:

IF THEY ARE MAINLY STOCKBROKERS, PILOTS, RUGBY PLAYERS, ACTORS, WATER RATS, CRICKETERS, HOTEL MANAGERS,

AND ALL OTHER KINDS OF
TAX-EVADING
DRUNKS...

GO TO ⟹ SEALED SECTION AT THE BACK AND TO HELL WITH IT!
OR PLAY IT SAFE AND GO TO: [D] or [E]

Core of speech:

NOTE: *if you don't know the guests or if you have no special message or have no time to write one, this section is an instant, generalised centrepiece to fill in the core of the Bookspeech.*

The Nearham Rotary Club

Two hours

NOTE: *use this section only if you are not known too well by the guest of honour or the group.*

The Rotarians

He/she/you/they – er – YOU
were founded in 1932

you
are a fraternity of formidable fund-raisers

you
promote goodwill and good fellowship everywhere!

You're

Bookspeech topic

I AM PARTICULARLY GRATIFIED TO HAVE BEEN CHOSEN TO SPEAK ON THIS OCCASION BECAUSE I HAVE KNOWN (insert name)

....

FOR WELL OVER (look at watch) ....

....

AND THAT'S A *LONG TIME TO TAKE* — ER — SO MUCH *ENORMOUS* PLEASURE IN SUCH HIGHLY *ESTEEMED, PEERLESS* AND *DISTINGUISHED* COMPANY! (YOU MAY WELL ASK, WHAT IS THIS CRAWLER *DOING* HERE?)

Optional insert
WELL, AFTER ALL, I DO HAVE A SPECIAL PERSONAL KNOWLEDGE OF (insert name)

....

YES, INDEED!
I KNOW THAT ....

....

I KNOW THAT ....

....

....

I KNOW THAT ....

....

....

I *KNOW* ALL THIS!
THE ONLY THING IS, ...
WONDERING WHO THE HELL *I* AM!

Guest

Guests

the Nearham Rotary Club

NOTE: I *have outlined nine arbitrary* qualities *that might be* typical *of our honoured guest, be he fund-raiser, company executive, bridegroom, female committee member, or both.* You *have to choose the ones that are likely to produce the most fun at your gathering. I have linked them with apposite groups of jokes and quotations.* You *can use them or put in your own. I suggest that three or four of the qualities are enough for a tight speech.* You *choose. Or use them all and see what happens!*

Rotarian

he

he

Brent Education Committee

BUT THAT IS WHAT *DEMOCRACY* IS ALL ABOUT! THAT I, A HUMBLE .... SHOULD BE CHOSEN TO SPEAK FOR ALL THE OTHER, LESS HUMBLE .... YOU SEE BEFORE YOU!

BUT LET THERE BE NO MISTAKE! THOUGH I STAND HERE, THE VERY *APOTHEOSIS* (AND I CHOOSE MY WORDS CAREFULLY EVEN IF I DON'T KNOW WHAT THEY MEAN!) OF *HUMILITY*, I AM PROUD TO POSE THE QUESTION:
'WHY IS ....

....
SO UNIVERSALLY RESPECTED? WHY?'
I REALLY CAN'T THINK OF ANY REASON – ER – WHY NOT.

Option if you wish to shorten speech

GO TO [⇒] [J9-1] THEN TO [F]

BUT PERHAPS THE REASON WILL BECOME CLEAR AS WE TRY TO DEFINE THE *INDEFINABLE* QUALITIES THAT *EXEMPLIFY* OUR – ER – *EXEMPLARY* ....
....

FIRST AND FOREMOST, ...
IS *FAR* TOO

HONEST!

AND THAT IS BECAUSE .... IS A DEMOCRAT, A PATRIOT, AND AT LEAST AS DEDICATED TO FREEDOM OF SPEECH AS ANY PAID-UP MEMBER OF (topical line) ....
....

GO TO [⇒] [Q2-1] MARK TWAIN OR TO [J1]

Rotarian

He

Rotarian
he

Edwina Curry

Ken Livingstone

34

SO THERE IS NO QUESTION THAT OUR FLAWLESS ....

....

IS HONEST! BUT THERE IS MORE TO HONESTY THAN MERELY TELLING THE TRUTH! .... KNOWS WHEN *NOT* TO TELL IT! THAT IS, WHEN TO BE:

TACTFUL

THOUGH THE NOBLEST DISPOSITION YOU
   INHERIT
AND YOUR CHARACTER WITH PIETY IS
   PACKED
ALL SUCH QUALITIES HAVE VERY LITTLE
   MERIT
UNACCOMPANIED BY TACT.

(Harry Graham)

GO TO ⟹ J2

THEN AGAIN, YOU ONLY HAVE TO MENTION OUR ARCHETYPAL .... TO BE TOLD THAT .... IS INCREDIBLY

BRAINY

NIMBLE-WITTED! ASTUTE! CIRCUMSPECT! ERUDITE ENOUGH TO ARGUE ON A SERIOUS, PHILOSOPHICAL LEVEL WORTHY OF HEGEL, SPINOZA AND .... AND SMART ENOUGH NEVER TO BUY A USED CAR FROM ....

GO TO ⟹ J3

Rotarian

he

your average Rotarian
twenty-five
he
he

Rotary

Rotarian

AND THOUGH OUR QUINTESSENTIAL ....
PURSUES TRUTH AND JUSTICE WITH ALL
THE FEROCIOUS ZEAL (AND TEETH) OF
ESTHER RANTZEN, IS .... NOT ALSO

TOLERANT?

TO THE POINT OF NEVER POINTING THE
FINGER? HOW RARE THAT IS! NEVER TO
CAST THE FIRST STONE WHEN THERE ARE
SO MANY WORTHY TARGETS!

GO TO  J4

HOW MAY WE EVEN *BEGIN* TO COMPRE-
HEND THAT ....
HAS BEEN *AT* IT FOR .... YEARS? I
MEAN, HOW DOES .... *DO* IT?
AND HOW DOES .... *KEEP* DOING
IT? AND HOW DO *WE* GET TO DO IT?
EVEN *HALF* OF IT? THE ANSWER IS *WE* HAVE
TO BE:

DYNAMIC!

FOR THAT IS WHAT ....: IS ALL ABOUT!

GO TO  J5

IT IS ONE THING TO BE DRIVEN, WITHOUT
NECESSARILY KNOWING WHAT DRIVES
YOU – LIKE A PASSENGER IN A BOMBAY
TAXI! BUT OUR INTREPID ....
DOES NOT RUSH IN WHERE DOG-BREEDERS
FEAR TO TREAD! OH, NO! SEE THAT NOBLE
NOSTRIL QUIVER, AS THE KEYNOTE OF
THE:

CAUTIOUS!

GO TO J6

NOTE: *save this one for the family tippler, the club boozer, the company drunk: if there isn't one, leave it out!*

Rotarian

guest

guest
he

dinner

John Smith, a gentleman

Rotarian

his

OF ONE THING WE CAN BE SURE! THERE IS NO PLACE *HERE* FOR FACETIOUS AND PETTY INNUENDOS ABOUT BOOZE AND WILD LIVING! OUR IRREPROACHABLE

....

IS, AT ALL TIMES

SOBER!

I WOULD NOT INSULT YOU *OR* YOUR

....

(look at audience) – I WOULD NOT INSULT YOUR .... WITH QUIPS SO TRIVIAL AS, FOR EXAMPLE: ' .... HAD ONLY *ONE* DRINK ALL THROUGH .... – A JUG OF ROUGH CIDER AND A STRAW!'
I MEAN, I REFUSE TO CRACK ANYTHING SO *CORNY* IN THE PRESENCE OF A *PARAGON* SUCH AS ....

....

WHOSE MYRIAD FACETS CORUSCATE INTO A BLAZE OF PHANTASMAGORIA – BEAMING UP INTO THE REALMS OF SUPRA-NATIONAL POSTERITY IN ONE DAZZLING *ZIG-ZAG* LINE!

GO TO ⟹ J7

AND THERE IS MORE!
HERE TODAY, IN HUMOURING – *HONOUR-ING* – OUR VERY MODEL OF A MODERN ......

....

WE ARE CONCERNED TO ILLUMINATE THE *TRUE* QUALITY OF .... *INDISPUTABLE* EMINENCE IN THE FIELD OF HUMAN CONQUEST, AND THAT MEANS:

SEXY!

your typical club member
he
boy

him
women

your average Rotary Club member

he

Rotarian

him .... *Mr*
he .... *his*
he
he
he
he
he

YES! PHYSICALLY ATTRACTIVE! WELL,
JUST LOOK AT ....
IT IS NOT JUST THAT .... IS A
GOOD-LOOKING .... WITH MUSCLES
– AND *HAIR* – A LOT OF US HAVE THAT – (to
him who is bald) – *HAD* THAT. NO, IT IS THE
EXTRA INGREDIENT, THE POWERFUL
ANIMAL *MAGNETISM* THAT MAKES ....
IRRESISTIBLE TO .... AND MAKES
THE REST OF THE SEX GRIND THEIR TEETH
IN – ADMIRATION! WELL, IF YOU'VE GOT
IT, *FLAUNT* IT! WHY NOT? AS SHAKESPEARE
MIGHT HAVE PUT IT BUT DIDN'T: 'WHAT IS
VIRTUE BUT INSUFFICIENT TEMPTATION?'

GOT TO ⟹ J8

ANYWAY, THERE WE ARE!

....
EPITOMISED IN A NUTSHELL OF COMMEND-
ABLE QUALITIES. HONEST, TOLERANT,
SOBER, WE COULD GO *ON* – BUT LET US
MERELY SAY THAT .... IS
ABOVE ALL:

HUMAN

YES! OUR EXEMPLARY ....
IS ONE OF *US*! A HUMAN BEING (POOR
THING!) YOU COULD ALMOST CALL ....
.... AVERAGE
CITIZEN! .... PAYS ALL .... TAXES
(...................................... HAS A NERVOUS AC-
COUNTANT): .... NEVER
EXCEEDS THE SPEED LIMIT: ....NEVER
PARKS ILLEGALLY: .... NEVER
CAUSES OBSTRUCTIONS: AND ....
NEVER WASTES PUBLIC TIME AND MONEY
BY PLEADING NOT GUILTY! ONE HUNDRED
PER CENT *HUMAN*!

GO TO ⟹ J9-1 (SOCKS ON)

E *Core of speech:*

NOTE: *if you have a personal knowledge of the guest of honour or group; if there is a special message, plea or tribute to be made; then you can research and write your own material for this specific centrepiece at the core of the Bookspeech.*

After the generalised opening here, there are blank pages against which I have set a brief example.

people

the annual Nearham Rotary Club awards

Los Angeles

London

Mr Moody,

London,
Mr John Smith, of Nearham Rotary Club.

John Smith.

your special topic

WELL, HERE WE ARE THEN! AND MAY I
JUST SAY, AS I GAZE AROUND AT THIS FINE
BODY OF MEN . . .
(assuming it isn't a stag party)
. . . THAT THERE ARE SOME FINE BODIES ON
THE WOMEN TOO . . . WHAT I MEAN IS, I CAN
NOT GET MY EYES – ER – MIND OFF THE
OUTSTANDING QUALITIES OF OUR GUEST(S)
OF HONOUR.

GO TO ⟶ J9-1 (SOCKS ON)

NOW PERHAPS, YOU HAVE SOME IDEA OF
THE KIND OF .... WE
ARE GATHERED HERE TO ROAST – TOAST.
WHICH BRINGS ME TO ....
....

AND *MY* REASON FOR BEING HERE.
I WAS IN ....
A FEW DAYS AGO, FINISHING MY NEW
NOVEL – I'M A VERY SLOW READER –
WHEN I GOT THIS LONG DISTANCE CALL
FROM ....
....
THE OPERATOR SAID: 'ER ....
....
I HAVE A LONG DISTANCE CALL FROM ......
....
A ....
....
WILL YOU PLEASE ACCEPT A REVERSE
CHARGE CALL?
SO HERE I AM, THANKS TO ....
ENJOYING THE WONDERFUL EIGHT
COURSE MEAL, SEVEN BAKED BEANS AND
A FINGER BOWL – IN THIS FINE RES-
TAURANT, WHERE THE FOOD IS ENTIRELY
UNTOUCHED BY HUMAN HANDS – THE
COOK IS AN ORANG-UTANG.

NOTE: *now you're on your own. Write (in pencil) on the other side, or clip in typed pages (cut down to this size). Meanwhile, here is an example:*

AND IT IS MY VERY GREAT PLEASURE TO PRESENT YOUR *ANNUAL HUMANITARIAN AWARD* TO THE NEARHAM ROTARIAN WHO HAS BEEN JUDGED BY THE COMMITTEE TO HAVE DONE THE MOST TO PROMOTE FRIENDSHIP AND UNDERSTANDING, AND TO BREAK DOWN BARRIERS OF FEAR, IGNORANCE AND PREJUDICE, BETWEEN THE MULTINATIONAL AND ETHNICALLY DIVERSE GROUPS IN THE NEARHAM DISTRICT.

WHAT REALLY INTRIGUES ME ABOUT THIS CONFLUENCE OF CHARITABLE CONCEPTS IS THAT WE ALL HAVE ONE THING IN COMMON – THE DEFINITION, DEVALUATION AND DESTRUCTION OF *PREJUDICE*. PROBABLY ADAM'S OLDEST CURSE FROM THE MOMENT HE SAW EVE AND SHE WAS *DIFFERENT*. IN THAT CASE, OF COURSE, 'VIVE LA DIFFÉRENCE'; BUT 'À BAS LE PRÉJUDICE!'

GO TO ⟹ J4

HOWEVER! THE NOMINEES FOR THE HUMANITARIAN AWARD ARE:

J. BOGGS
P. FULLER
Z. PENGALLION

AND THE WINNER IS:

PRESENT THE PRIZE AND

GO TO ⟹ F (PERORATION)

Your version here

NOTE: *the peroration or winding-up may include gags or, if you've roasted your victim(s) enough, it must be a sincere and genuine tribute, in your own words.*

John Smith and your happy band of Nearham Rotarians

another wonderful year ahead, another superb dinner like this one, and, as far as I am concerned humanitarian awards for every single one of you!

Peroration

AND SO, MY DEAR ....
....
....
....

MAY I, ON BEHALF OF MYSELF, THE
GUESTS, TWO WAITERS AND A DISH-
WASHER, WISH YOU ....
....
....
....
....
....

END SPEECH HERE

OR

CONTINUE FOR TOASTS

AND MAY I SEND YOU ALL ON YOUR WAY
WITH A SINCERE AND AFFECTIONATE
TOAST FROM THOSE OF US WHO HAVE TO
STAY BEHIND TO DO THE WASHING UP.

GO TO [⟹] T TOASTS

Appendices

Appendices?
Those little
bits extra on
the end?
I'll take as
many as you
can get!

MAE
WEST

Appendix

NOTE: *this is a reference section for section A. There you can pencil in the chosen allocution and opening remarks from here.*

This is a very brief list of correct forms, and clerks and secretaries of companies will always advise on the form of address and the speaking order and length of time desired.

NOTE: *precedence: order is 1–2–3–4, except chairman is always first unless royalty is present.*

NOTE: *precedence at a wedding always distinguishes the host and hostess, who are paying for it.*

Openers

O1 | Allocutions or forms of address

O1-1 | Royalty
WHEN THE QUEEN OR QUEEN MOTHER
IS PRESENT:
'MAY IT PLEASE YOUR MAJESTY, (MR
CHAIRMAN, ETC...)'
FOR PRINCE PHILIP AND OTHER ROYALS:
'MAY IT PLEASE YOUR ROYAL HIGHNESS,'

O1-2 | Peerage and knights

DUKE	YOUR GRACE
MARQUESS	MY LORD
VISCOUNT	MY LORD
BARON	MY LORD
DUCHESS	YOUR GRACE
MARCHIONESS	MY LADY
VISCOUNTESS	MY LADY
BARONESS	MY LADY
BARONET	SIR
KNIGHT	SIR JOHN SMITH

O1-3 | Church

ALL ARCHBISHOPS	YOUR GRACE
ALL BISHOPS	BISHOP
THE POPE	YOUR HOLINESS
CARDINAL	YOUR EMINENCE

O1-4 | Civic

LORD MAYOR	MY LORD MAYOR
LADY MAYORESS	MY LADY MAYORESS
MAYOR OF CITY	MR MAYOR
A LADY MAYOR	MADAM MAYOR
CHAIRMAN OF COMPANY	MR CHAIRMAN
LADY CHAIRMAN	MADAM CHAIRMAN

O1-5 | Wedding
BRIDE AND BRIDEGROOM, HOST AND
HOSTESS, PARENTS OF THE GROOM,
REVEREND SIR, LADIES AND GENTLEMEN.

John Smith

Nearham

Nearham

NOTE: *when addressing a society or company known by its initials there is some fun to be had in reinterpreting them e.g., 'NATO which means "No Action, Talk Only"' but I wouldn't use it at a NATO conference.*

O2 *Funny starters*

O2-1 *False wedding starter*

BRIDE, BRIDEGROOM – OH, I BEG YOUR PARDON, WRONG DAY – ER – LADIES AND GENTLEMEN, ESTEEMED GUESTS AND

....

....

O2-2 *Sporting occasion*

MR SPORTING PRESIDENT, FELLOW SPORT-ING MEMBERS, SPORTING GUEST OF HONOUR, SPORTING LADIES AND GENTLE-MEN, (CAMP) SPORTS (DEEP VOICE) AND JUST TO MAKE SURE NOBODY FEELS LEFT OUT, CADS, BOUNDERS AND SNEAKS! (OR, IF YOU'RE AMERICAN, FINKS!)

O2-3 *Gefüllte fish*

LADIES AND GENTLEMEN OF ....

....

MAY I SAY HOW PLEASED AND PROUD I AM TO HAVE BEEN CHOSEN, ON THIS VERY *SPECIAL* OCCASION, TO ADDRESS *YOU*, THE CREAM, THE CAVIARE, THE VERY GE-FÜLLTE FISH OF ....

....

SOCIETY. FUNNY, THE LAST TIME I SAID 'GEFÜLLTE FISH' ONLY ONE MAN LAUGHED – AND HE WAS AN ARAB.

O2-4 *Initials*

MR CHAIRMAN, LADIES AND GENTLEMEN OF THE IMF, WHICH, AS WE ALL KNOW, MEANS: 'I MOVE FAST'..,
OR
MR CHAIRMAN, LADIES AND GENTLEMEN OF THE BBC, MEANING 'BEST BEFORE CHRISTMAS'...

O2-5 *Stag Party*

LADIES AND GENTLEMEN, OH, SORRY, THERE ARE NO *LADIES*! GENTLEMEN!... OH, SORRY, THERE ARE NONE OF *THOSE* HERE EITHER. WELL, LISTEN YOU LOT!

John Smith

O2-6 Lucky kiss

THERE IS A TRADITION THAT WHEN A BABY IS BORN IT IS KISSED BY ITS GUARDIAN ANGEL FOR LUCK. IF THE BABY IS KISSED ON THE HEAD, IT BECOMES A GREAT THINKER, IF ON THE HANDS, A GREAT ARTIST, IF ON THE MOUTH, A GREAT ORATOR. I DON'T KNOW WHERE

....

WAS KISSED, BUT HE CERTAINLY MAKES A GREAT CHAIRMAN.

O2-7 Brevity

THE LORD'S PRAYER HAS 56 WORDS; THE TEN COMMANDMENTS HAVE 297; THE AMERICAN DECLARATION OF INDEPENDENCE HAS 300 WORDS. BUT A CIVIL SERVANT DIRECTIVE ON THE IMPORT OF SPLINTER-FREE TOILET TISSUE HAS 36,479! THE MORAL IS PLAIN; I SHALL BE BRIEF.

O2-8 Bull

CONFUCIUS, HE SAY, MAN MAKING SPEECH IS LIKE TOREADOR FACING HORNS; POINT HERE, POINT THERE, AND AWFUL LOT OF BULL IN THE MIDDLE.

Reader's notes for O

Appendix J

NOTE: *the first nine categories of jokes in this appendix have been tested in the context of the nine qualities of section* D. *Thus, if you choose TACTFUL as a quality of your guest, you can use any of the jokes in* J2 , *TALES FOR THE TACTFUL, and thereby integrate them in the Bookspeech.*

It is not enough just to tell jokes, *you must tie them in, relate them to the audience. You can pretend that some of them are true stories about the guests, you can put in their names, make up names for their 'ancestors', e.g. 'Sir Phineas' or 'Lady Partridge'.*

Learn how to switch a joke to make it fit. I have given an example on J9-1 , *and hinted at switches for other jokes.*

When you add your own favourite, try to place it in the appropriate subdivision of J ; *it will fit somewhere, even if you have to squeeze it a bit.*

Jokes

J1 Tales for the honest

J1-1 Trust

FOR WHAT *IS* HONESTY? AND *WHERE* IS IT WITHOUT *TRUST*? WHERE, INDEED, IS THERE A FINER EXAMPLE OF HONESTY THAN THE ROMAN CATHOLIC CONFESSIONAL, WHERE ONE MAN ENTRUSTS HIS INNERMOST SECRETS TO ANOTHER?

CAN YOU BELIEVE THAT TWO YOUNG THUGS COULD BE PERSUADED TO TRUST THEIR LOCAL PRIEST ENOUGH TO MAKE A JOINT CONFESSIONAL, AT THE *SAME TIME*, ONE *EACH SIDE* OF HIM? THAT THEY COULD TELL IT *ALL*, EVERYTHING EXCEPT MURDER, AND EVEN *THAT* TREMBLING ON THE NEW-FOUND HONESTY OF THEIR LIPS?

AND THAT WHEN THE PRIEST WAS CALLED AWAY ON URGENT PARISH BUSINESS AND HAD TO LEAVE THE BOX, THE TWO TRUSTING FELONS WAITED THERE FOR A FULL *FIFTEEN* MINUTES BEFORE ONE OF THEM SHOUTED: 'COME ON, DANNY, LET'S GET OUTA HERE, HE'S BLOODY GONE FOR THE POLICE!'

J1-2 Alligator

LOOK AT YOUR LOCAL DOCTOR .... WHO IS NOTORIOUS FOR SAYING EXACTLY WHAT HE THINKS. A PATIENT CAME INTO HIM ONE DAY WEARING A FACE MASK.

'TAKE THAT SILLY THING OFF!' SAID THE DOCTOR. (Muffled) ' I HAVE BAD BREATH,' SAID THE MAN. 'CAN'T BE THAT BAD,' SAID THE DOCTOR, 'TAKE IT OFF!'

THE MAN TOOK OFF THE MASK AND BREATHED AND THE DOCTOR FELL OVER.

'PUT IT BACK!' HE SAID, 'AND EAT A POUND OF ALLIGATOR DROPPINGS.'

(Muffled) 'ALLIGATOR DROPPINGS!' SAID THE MAN, 'WHAT GOOD WILL *THAT* DO?'

'NOT MUCH,' SAID THE DOCTOR, 'BUT IT'LL TONE IT DOWN A BIT.'

Marvin Rose, a member of Rotary

Marvin

Marvin

J2 *Tales for the tactful*

J2-1 *Salesman*

I MEAN, THERE IS A TALE THEY TELL OF

....

WHO CLOSED HIS SHOP FRIDAY NIGHT AND RUSHED TO THE TEMPLE FOR THE SABBATH SERVICE. HE RUSHED SO FAST HE LEFT SOMETHING UNDONE – HIS *ZIP*!

AT THE ENTRANCE, HE MET BERTHA BROWNE, THE PRESIDENT OF THE LADIES' GUILD.

'I DON'T LIKE TO SAY NOTHING,' SHE SAID SHYLY, WAVING A TACTFUL FINGER DOWNWARDS, BUT YOUR – ER – *BUSINESS* IS OPEN.'

'YOU'RE MISTAKEN, LADY.'

'BELIEVE ME,' SAID MRS BROWNE, BLUSH-ING AND POINTING THE TACTFUL FINGER, 'YOUR – ER – *BU-SI-NESS* IS *OPEN*!

'HOW DARE YOU!' SHOUTED .... RUSHING INSIDE.'I'M *NEVER* OPEN SHABB-OS, I CLOSE THE STORE EVERY FRIDAY TO COME HERE!' BUT LATER ON, INSIDE,

....

SAW THAT HIS ZIP WAS OPEN AND REALISED MRS BROWN WAS BEING TACT-FUL. HE WENT TO HER AT ONCE.

'MRS BROWNE,' HE SAID, 'I WANT TO APOLOGISE.' THEN, ALSO WAVING THE TACTFUL FINGER, HE SAID: 'BUT TELL ME SOMETHING. WHEN MY *BU-SI-NESS* WAS *O-PEN* . . . WAS MY *SALESMAN IN* OR *OUT*?'

HIDE YOUR HEAD IN SHAME

AND CREEP BACK TO ☐ ⟹ D

OR DON'T TELL THIS JOKE.
TURN THE PAGE AND TELL THE UNCIR-CUMCISED VERSION OF THE TACTFUL TALE.

The wife of the chairman...

WHEN IT COMES TO TACT, ...
....
TAKES SOME BEATING. THE LOCAL VICAR CALLS ON HER ONE DAY, HEARS MUSIC BLARING IN THE HOUSE, KNOCKS ON THE DOOR... AND NOBODY ANSWERS. SO HE LEAVES HIS VISITING CARD WITH A MESSAGE ON THE BACK: 'REVELATIONS 3: 20; "BEHOLD, I STAND AT THE DOOR, AND KNOCK: IF ANY MAN HEAR MY VOICE, AND OPEN THE DOOR, I WILL COME IN TO HIM...'

WHAT DOES SHE DO?

THE FOLLOWING SUNDAY, AFTER MORNING SERVICE, SHE SLIPS AN ENVELOPE INTO THE VICAR'S HAND AND DISAPPEARS BEFORE HE CAN OPEN HIS MOUTH. SO HE OPENS THE LETTER AND READS: 'GENESIS 3: 10; "I HEARD THY VOICE IN THE GARDEN, AND I WAS AFRAID, BECAUSE I WAS NAKED, AND I HID MYSELF."'

NOW HIDE YOUR HEAD IN PENITENCE

AND KNEEL BACK TO ⟹ D

the chairman of Rotary

Leslie Crowther

Cyrus Smith

J3 *Tales for the brainy*

J3-1 *E I E I O*

DID YOU KNOW THAT ....
WAS ONE OF THE FIRST CONTESTANTS ON
'MASTERMIND'? MAGNUS MAGNUSSON
ASKED HIM TO COMPLETE THE LINE OF A
SONG: 'OLD MACDONALD HAD A . . .'

AND THE ANSWER CAME: 'FARM!'

'CORRECT!' SAID MAGNUS MAGNUSSON,
'NOW *SPELL* THE WORD "FARM" . . .'

AND THE ANSWER CAME: 'E I E I O!'

IF THEY LAUGH AT THAT,

GO BACK TO ⟩ D

IF THE JOKE DIES, SAY: 'THAT JOKE WAS
GIVEN TO ME BY ....
AND WAS HE GLAD TO GET RID OF IT!'

AND GO TO ⟩ F

J3-2 *Taste*

IF THERE IS ONE MAN WHO *REALLY*
UNDERSTANDS PEOPLE, THAT IS PROFES-
SOR ....
WHO OCCUPIES THE CHAIR OF SOCIAL
PSYCHOLOGY AT BIRKBECK. A STUDENT
CAME TO HIM FOR ADVICE. 'PROFESSOR',
HE SAID, 'EVERY GIRL I BRING HOME, MY
MOTHER *HATES*! THEY'RE TOO FAT OR TOO
THIN OR TOO CLEVER OR TOO STUPID OR
TOO MOUSEY OR TOO NOISY. NOBODY IS
GOOD ENOUGH.'

THE PROFESSOR SMILED. 'FIND A YOUNG
WOMAN WHO LOOKS LIKE YOUR MOTHER,'
HE SAID. '*SHE'LL* BE GOOD ENOUGH.'

A MONTH LATER, THE STUDENT CAME
FOR HIS TUTORIAL. 'PROFESSOR', HE SAID,
'I DID IT! I FOUND A GIRL WHO NOT ONLY
LOOKS LIKE MY MOTHER, SHE HAS THE
SAME VOICE, THE SAME PERSONALITY,
THE SAME *MIND*!'

THE PROFESSOR SMILED. 'WELL, THEN?'
'MY *FATHER* HATES HER.'

your average Rotarian

Riddle

THAT IS WHY ....
LOVES BRAIN-TEASERS AND RIDDLES. LIKE
THIS ONE: A DEMOCRATIC MARXIST, AN
INEXPENSIVE BUILDER, SANTA CLAUS
AND A JESUIT PRIEST SEE A PRETTY GIRL
PASS BY. WHICH ONE WINKS AT HER?

IT HAS TO BE THE JESUIT PRIEST,
BECAUSE THE OTHERS ARE FIGMENTS OF
THE IMAGINATION.

NOTE: *you may tell these jokes singly or one after the other, whichever best suits the occasion.*

club
Smith-Reilly

NOTE: *whoever tells this will put his own religion last. It's what you might call... a point of view?... ethnic bias?... team spirit?... a little sad?*

J4 Tales for the tolerant

J4-1 Jump!

WE ONLY HAVE TO TURN TO THE IRISH SIDE OF THE .... AND LOOK AT FATHER BRENDAN ....

HE SAW A MAN ABOUT TO JUMP FROM THE TOP OF A HIGH BUILDING. 'DON'T JUMP, MAN,' HE SHOUTED, 'FOR GOD'S SAKE!'

'I'M JUMPIN' FOR MY SAKE! HE SHOUTED.

'THEN DON'T JUMP FOR THE SAKE OF ST PETER AND THE MOST HOLY SAINTS!'

'I'M NOT STOPPIN' THEM FROM JUMPIN',' SHOUTED THE MAN.

'THEN I SAY TO YOU: DON'T JUMP FOR THE SAKE OF THE MOST HOLY VIRGIN.'

'WHO'S THE MOST HOLY VIRGIN?' SHOUTED THE MAN. AND FATHER BRENDAN SHOUTED: 'JUMP, YOU DIRTY PROTESTANT, JUMP!'

NOW, I SUPPOSE I'D BETTER PUT IT RIGHT WITH THE CATHOLICS.

J4-2 Brick

IN BELFAST, THERE IS A SHOP THAT SELLS CATHOLIC BOOKS AND CATHOLIC STATUES AND CATHOLIC SACRED HEARTS AND ALL THINGS CATHOLIC, AND A PROTESTANT THREW A BRICK THROUGH THE WINDOW, SHOUTING: 'JESUS CHRIST, I CAN'T STAND ALL THIS BLOODY INTOLERANCE!'

J4-3 Wishes

A CATHOLIC PRIEST, A PROTESTANT MINISTER AND A RABBI WENT TO HEAVEN. THE GUARDIAN APPEARED AND SAID: 'AS A REWARD FOR YOUR SELFLESS LIVES YOU ARE EACH GRANTED ONE WISH.'

THE CATHOLIC SAID: 'I WISH THERE WERE NO PROTESTANTS LEFT ON EARTH.'

THE MINISTER SAID: 'I WISH THERE WERE NO CATHOLICS.' 'NOW YOU, RABBI', SAID THE GUARDIAN, 'WHY ARE YOU SILENT?'

THE RABBI SHOOK HIS HEAD. 'I HAVE NOTHING TO ASK,' HE SAID. 'JUST GRANT THEM THEIR WISHES.'

Smith of Nearham

Arthur Scargill
SDP

REMEMBER WHAT HAPPENED TO ALBERT

WHO WAS SHIPWRECKED ON A DESERT ISLAND FOR TWENTY YEARS: (HE PRAYED EVERY DAY, OBSERVED ALL THE FESTIVALS, KEPT A KOSHER KITCHEN... I MERELY MENTION THESE DETAILS IN CASE THERE ARE ANY THEOLOGICAL STUDENTS PRESENT) UNTIL ONE DAY HE WAS RESCUED BY A PASSING SHIP.

'TELL ME,' SAID THE CAPTAIN, 'WHAT DID YOU *DO* FOR TWENTY YEARS? DID YOU LIVE LIKE ROBINSON CRUSOE?'

'CRUSOE SHMUSOE,' SAID ALBERT, 'I WENT INTO THE BUILDING BUSINESS.' AND HE TOOK THE CAPTAIN TO A CORNER OF THE ISLAND AND SHOWED HIM A BEAUTIFUL SYNAGOGUE.

'INCREDIBLE,' SAID THE CAPTAIN, 'YOU DID THIS ENTIRELY BY YOURSELF?'

'THAT'S NOTHING!' SAID ALBERT, AND TOOK HIM TO THE *OTHER* CORNER OF THE ISLAND AND SHOWED HIM *ANOTHER* BEAUTIFUL SYNAGOGUE.

'WHY?' SAID THE CAPTAIN, 'YOU'RE THE ONLY ONE ON THE ISLAND! WHY DID YOU BUILD TWO SYNAGOGUES?'

'*THIS* ONE IS *ORTHODOX*,' SAID ALBERT. 'THE *OTHER* IS *REFORM*. *THIS* ONE I *BELONG* TO: THE OTHER ONE, I WOULDN'T SET FOOT IN IF THEY *PAID* ME!'

AS I GAZE AROUND, I REALISE I MAY HAVE TOLD THE WRONG JOKE. NEXT TIME I'LL MAKE IT TWO CHURCHES! AND THE WAY THINGS ARE GOING HERE, IT'LL SOON BE TWO MOSQUES. ANYWAY, IT WAS THINKING LIKE THAT THAT LED TO THE GREAT SCHISM, THE REFORMATION, CALVIN, LUTHER ....
AND THE ....

NOT THAT I'M PREJUDICED... I HATE *EVERYBODY* IRRESPECTIVE OF RACE, NATIONALITY, COLOUR OR CREED. I SHOULD HAVE BEEN A JOURNALIST.

IF YOU WRIGGLE OUT OF THAT ONE

GO BACK TO ⟹ WHERE YOU CAME FROM.

Sir Cedric Smith, the great grandfather of the first chairman of Rotary,

J5 *Tales for the dynamic*

J5-1 *Lumberjack*

DYNAMIC MEN TEND TO FOUND DYN-
ASTIES OF DYNAMIC DESCENDANTS.
THERE'S A LUMBERJACK CAMP IN THE
YUKON WHERE THEY STILL TALK ABOUT
THE DAY ....

....

ARRIVED. HE WAS TERRIBLY POLITE,
TERRIBLY TIDY AND TERRIBLY ENGLISH.

'CHOPPING MY WAY ROUND THE
WORLD,' HE SAID, 'AND I'D LIKE A JOB.'

THE LUMBERJACKS ROARED. 'GIVE THE
LIMEY A MEAT-AXE,' SAID THE BOSS, 'AND
TWO HOURS TO CHOP DOWN THE SMALL-
EST TREE.'

THE ENGLISHMAN TOOK THE AXE,
FLICKED HIS WRIST AND THE SAPLING
WAS DOWN. 'WISE GUY, EH?' SAID THE
BOSS, AND HE GAVE HIM A GIANT AXE AND
SHOWED HIM THE BIGGEST REDWOOD IN
THE FOREST. 'YOU WANNA JOB?' HE SAID,
'CUT THAT DOWN!'

THE ENGLISHMAN TOOK THE AXE, SPAT
ON EACH PALM, AND WITH TWO FLICKS OF
THE WRIST, SENT THE HUGE TREE CRASH-
ING TO EARTH. THE BIG GUYS STARED IN
WONDER.

'WHERE THE HELL YOU FROM?' SAID THE
BOSS.

'THE SAHARA DESERT,' SAID THE LITTLE
MAN.

'C'MON,' SAID THE BOSS, 'THERE AIN'T
NO TREES IN THE SAHARA!'

'NOT ANY MORE,' HE SAID.

the grandfather of the first chairman of Rotary

the grandfather of the first chairman of Rotary,

The soldier

FOR SHEER DYNAMISM, NOBODY COULD EQUAL ALEXANDER, ...
....

HE RULED HIS FATHER'S TIMBER BUSINESS LIKE AN EMPEROR, AND YET, DURING THE WAR, INSISTED ON JOINING THE ARMY, DISDAINED A COMMISSION, AND SERVED IN THE RANKS. THEN ONE DAY HE HAD TO REPORT SICK WITH GASTRIC FLU. 'STOMACH ACHE?' SNEERED THE POMPOUS LITTLE MEDICAL OFFICER, 'WOULD YOU TAKE TIME OFF TO COME TO ME WITH STOMACH ACHE IN CIVIL LIFE?' 'NO,' SAID ALEXANDER, STIFFLY AT ATTENTION, 'I SHOULD *SEND* FOR YOU.'

The son

THE MIGHTY ALEXANDER, ...
....

HAD A SON. AS SOON AS THE BOY COULD UNDERSTAND, ALEXANDER TOOK HIM ON HIS KNEE AND SAID: 'ONE DAY, ALL THIS WILL BE YOURS: YOU, MY SON, WILL FOLLOW IN MY FOOTSTEPS!'

IN DUE COURSE, THE BOY BECAME A JUNIOR CLERK, WORKED HIS WAY UP TO HEAD OF INVESTMENT, MADE A KILLING ON THE STOCK EXCHANGE, HOLIDAYED ON HIS FATHER'S YACHT, SLEPT WITH HIS FATHER'S MISTRESS AND GAVE ORDERS WITH SUCH SUPER DYNAMISM THAT HE MADE POWERFUL ENEMIES.

HIS FATHER CALLED HIM IN.

'MY SON,' HE SAID, 'YOU ARE EXCEEDING YOUR AUTHORITY.'

'BUT PAPA,' SAID THE YOUTH, 'YOU WANT ME TO FOLLOW IN YOUR FOOTSTEPS.'

'YES,' SAID ALEXANDER, 'BUT GIVE ME TIME TO GET OUT OF THEM FIRST.'

the father of the first chairman of Rotary,

JULIUS, ...

DID NOT FOLLOW TOO WELL IN THE FOOTSTEPS OF HIS FATHER, THE TYCOON, ALEXANDER, WHO DIED HEARTBROKEN. JULIUS TOOK OVER THE BUSINESS, SQUANDERED A FORTUNE, MADE BAD DEALS AND WAS BOUGHT OUT BY HIS YOUNGER BROTHER JUST IN TIME TO SAVE THE FIRM.

SO JULIUS SPENT HIS TIME MARRYING RICH WIVES AND HITTING THE SUNDAY HEADLINES, A DISSOLUTE RAKE OF 68.

AND YET, ONE DAY WHEN A YOUNG MODEL FELL OVERBOARD FROM HIS YACHT, JULIUS WENT STRAIGHT OVER AFTER HER AND BROUGHT HER BACK. THE OLD FAMILY RETAINER WAS IN TEARS.

'AH, MASTER JULIUS, HOW PROUD YOUR DEAR FATHER WOULD HAVE BEEN THIS DAY!'

AND JULIUS SAID, 'WHO *PUSHED* ME?'

NOTE: *once again, flexibility is possible with this joke. It can be switched to any national or ethnic group to suit the audience.*

chairman's family

Smith-Williams

Smith-Williams

Smith-Williams

J6   *Tales for the cautious*

J6-1   *Welsh*

THEY'RE PARTICULARLY CAUTIOUS ON THE WELSH SIDE OF THE ....
I MEAN, YOU WOULDN'T *BELIEVE* DAI .... THE GRANDAD, WHO WAS MARRIED TO GRANDMA BLODWYN.

NOT LONG AFTER THEY GOT MARRIED IN THE RHONDDA, BLODWYN DIDN'T FEEL TOO GOOD SO SHE WENT TO SEE EVANS THE PILL. HE LOOKED HER OVER AND SAID: 'MRS ....
I AM VERY PLEASED TO TELL YOU, *SINCE* YOU ARE NICELY MARRIED, THAT YOU ARE PREGNANT.'

'PREGNANT!' SHRIEKED BLODWYN. 'OH, WAIT TILL I TELL DAI!'

SHE RUSHED HOME AND TELEPHONED THE PIT. 'I MUST SPEAK TO DAI .... AT ONCE,' SHE SHOUTED! 'I DON'T CARE IF HE *IS* AT THE PIT-FACE, TELL HIM IT'S VERY URGENT!' THE MESSAGE WENT DOWN THE MINE, VERY URGENT LIKE, AND DAI WAS TOLD HE BETTER GO UP, HE WAS WANTED ON THE PHONE VERY URGENT. SO DAI WENT UP THE LIFT NICE AND URGENT AND WENT TO THE TELE-PHONE AND SAID: 'ULLO'.

BLODWYN SHOUTED DOWN THE PHONE: 'DAI, I'M *PREGNANT*!' DEAD SILENCE FROM DAI.

'DAI, CAN'T YOU HEAR? I'M *PREGNANT*! WHY DON'T YOU *SAY* SOMETHING?'

AND DAI SAID: 'WHO'S SPEAKING?'

Rotary
OR family

BUT CAUTION IS A .... TRADITION. ONE ESTEEMED MEMBER, WHEN AWAY ON A BUSINESS TRIP, WOULD NEVER SEND MORE THAN A CRYPTIC CABLE HOME TO HIS WORRIED MOTHER.

IN JANUARY, HE CABLED: 'ALL'S WELL, CAUTION ADVISED, CAN ONLY SAY: SHOT POLAR BEAR YESTERDAY.'

IN JULY, HE CABLED: 'ALL'S WELL, CAUTION ADVISED, CAN ONLY SAY: DANCED WITH HULA-HULA GIRL LAST NIGHT.'

IN AUGUST, HE CABLED: 'IN HOSPITAL, NOT CAUTIOUS ENOUGH, DOCTOR SAYS SHOULD HAVE DANCED WITH POLAR BEAR AND SHOT HULA-HULA GIRL.'

Rotary Club

Sir Aubrey Smith

One noted Rotarian

J7 *Tales for the sober*

J7-1 *Dancer*

THERE ARE, ALAS, MANY SKELETONS IN THE .... CLOSET. A SENIOR MINISTER OF THE CROWN, THE HONOURABLE .... HAD BEEN STEADILY TANKING UP AT A BUCKINGHAM PALACE GARDEN PARTY. WHEN MUSIC STARTED, HE STAGGERED OVER TO A FIGURE IN RED. 'C'MON, YOU BEAU'FUL CREATURE, LE'S DANCE!'

'NO, NO AND *NO!*'

'WHA'DYA MEAN, NO, NO AN'*NO?*'

'NO BECAUSE *YOU* ARE DISGUSTINGLY DRUNK, NO, BECAUSE *THAT* IS THE NATIONAL ANTHEM, AND NO, BECAUSE *I* AM THE CARDINAL ARCHBISHOP!'

J7-2 *Double*

.... WENT INTO A PUB. 'WHAT WILL YOU HAVE?' SAID THE LANDLORD. 'LARGE WHISKY,' SAID THE MAN. THE LANDLORD ASKED FOR PAYMENT.

'OH, NO, NO, NO,' SAID THE MAN, 'DISTNC'LY R'MEMBER – *YOU* 'VITED ME T'AVE DRINK. VER' KIND OF YOU.'

ANOTHER CUSTOMER, WHO WAS A SOLICITOR CHIPPED IN. 'HE'S RIGHT, LANDLORD, THERE WAS AN OFFER AND ACCEPTANCE – THAT'S A CONTRACT.'

'THEN GET OUT,' SAID THE LANDLORD, 'AND DON'T *EVER* COME BACK!'

THE MAN WALKED OUT OF THE PUB AND CAME STRAIGHT BACK IN AGAIN. 'I THOUGHT I TOLD YOU NEVER TO COME BACK!' SAID THE LANDLORD.

'NEVER BEEN HERE I' MY LIFE BEFORE,' SAID THE MAN. 'REALLY?' SNORTED THE LANDLORD. 'THEN ALL I CAN SAY IS YOU MUST HAVE A DOUBLE!'

'DON' MIND IF I DO,' SAID THE MAN, 'AN' I'M SURE OUR SOLIC'TOR FRIEND WILL HAVE ONE TOO!'

Drunk?

'RETURN TICKET, PLEASE.' 'WHERE TO?' 'BACK HERE OF COURSE.'

'STOP DRINKING... WHAT DO YOU MEAN, YOU'RE PERFECTLY SOBER, YOUR FACE IS GETTING BLURRED.'

'I TAKE A DRINK NOW AND THEN TO STEADY MYSELF, BUT SOMETIMES I GET SO STEADY I CAN'T MOVE.'

Smythe
the founder of the club

J8 | Tales for the sexy

J8-1 | The stripper

THE TEMPTATION TO 'FLAUNT IT' IS AS OLD AS ADAM – OR EVE. THERE IS A LOT WHISPERED ABOUT LADY SIMONE .... A FOREBEAR OF .... AND A NOTABLE BEAUTY; AMONGST OTHER THINGS.

ONE EVENING, SHE RETURNED EARLY FROM THE HUNT BALL AND WENT STRAIGHT TO HER BEDROOM. ARMAND, HER HANDSOME FOOTMAN WAS RECLINING ON HER CHAISE LONGUE, SIPPING HER BEST CLARET. HE STOOD UP AND SMILED. SHE SMILED BACK.

'ARMAND,' SHE SAID, 'TAKE OFF MY SHOES.'

'OUI, MADAME,' HE SAID. AND HE DID.

'ARMAND, TAKE OFF MY COAT.'

'VERY GOOD, MADAME,' HE SAID, AND DID. SLOWLY.

'MY DRESS?'

'AVEC PLAISIR.' VERY SLOWLY.

'ARMAND, THE REST OF MY CLOTHES... EVERY... SINGLE... ONE.'

'EVERY... SINGLE... ONE... MADAME.' OH *SO* SLOWLY.

'YOU DID THAT BEAUTIFULLY, ARMAND. AND NOW... IF YOU WISH TO REMAIN IN MY SERVICE... YOU ARE NEVER TO WEAR MY CLOTHES AGAIN.'

J8-2 | The apple

AND AS ADAM MIGHT HAVE SAID TO EVE BUT DIDN'T: 'AFTER WE EAT THIS APPLE WE'RE GONNA DO *WHAT*?'

your chairman

ONLY LAST WEEK, THE SWINGING HEAD MISTRESS OF THE LOCAL GIRLS' SCHOOL ASKED .... TO TALK TO HER SIXTH FORMERS ABOUT SEX.

'ME, TALK ABOUT *SEX* TO *SIXTH FORMERS*,' HE SAID, '*HOW?*'

'THE GIRLS WILL *TAKE* IT FROM YOU,' SHE SAID, 'YOUR FACE HAS THAT "LIVED-IN-AND-LEFT-MOST-OF-IT-BEHIND" LOOK!'

ALL THE SAME HE WAS QUITE EMBARRASSED AND TOLD HIS *WIFE* THAT HE WAS GIVING A TALK TO THE GIRLS ABOUT *SAILING*, ON BEHALF OF THE LOCAL *YACHT* CLUB.

THE NEXT DAY HIS WIFE HAPPENED TO MEET THE HEAD MISTRESS.

'YOUR HUSBAND GAVE MY GIRLS A TERRIFIC TALK,' SHE SAID, 'HE *REALLY* KNOWS WHAT IT'S ALL ABOUT.'

THE WIFE LAUGHED. 'GREAT,' SHE SAID, 'BUT BETWEEN YOU AND ME, HE'S ONLY DONE IT TWICE; THE FIRST TIME HE WAS SICK, THE SECOND TIME, HIS HAT BLEW OFF!'

NOTE: *do not aim this joke directly at the guest of honour unless you know him well. If aimed at a woman, e.g. Bertha, make her the secretary.*

a former chairman of the Nearham Rotary Club

his secretary, Bertha

.

I retire as chairman

farewell
Bertha

Bertha

The Nearham Rotary Club, Jimmy Saville, and Princess Michael of Kent ... still selling books.

J9 | Tales for the human

J9-1 | Socks on

IN THIS CONTEXT, I REALLY MUST TELL
YOU ABOUT ....

....

WHO WENT TO HIS OFFICE ONE MORNING,
LOOKING VERY DEPRESSED. 'ANYTHING
WRONG, SIR?' SAID .... SWISHING
HER NYLONS AND CROSSING HER LEGS IN
A VERY UN-LIBERATED FASHION.

....

'TOMORROW,' HE SAID, 'AND NOBODY
GIVES A DAMN! NO PRESENTATION, NO
.... PARTY, NOTHING! SO MUCH
FOR MY "FRIENDS"!' ....
FLUTTERED HER LONG PRE-SEXIST EYE-
LASHES. 'WELL, WHY DON'T YOU HAVE A
PRIVATE PARTY WITH *ME* – TONIGHT –
HMMMM? COME TO MY FLAT ABOUT TEN
O'CLOCK? HMMMMMM?'

HE WAS THERE AT NINE FIFTY-FIVE,
IMMACULATELY DRESSED, SMOTHERED IN
BRUT, AND STUNNED AT THE SIGHT OF
.... IN A CLINGING, BLACK
DRESS AND LOOKING UNBELIEVABLY
RAVISHING!

'HAVE A DRINK,' SHE SAID, ' AND EXCUSE
ME WHILE I SLIP INTO . . . THE NEXT ROOM.'
THEN, A FEW MINUTES LATER, 'YOU CAN
COME IN NOW.'

HE OPENED THE DOOR AND GAZED UPON
THE MOST INCREDIBLE SIGHT HE HAD
EVER SEEN! ALL HIS COLLEAGUES WERE
THERE, HIS FELLOW JP'S, THE LOCAL MEM-
BER OF PARLIAMENT, THE ENTIRE MEM-
BERSHIP OF ....

....

....

ALL GATHERED ROUND A HUGE TABLE,
LOADED WITH CAVIARE, SMOKED SALMON,
CHAMPAGNE, PRESENTS, THE LOT! HIS
FRIENDS HAD *NOT* FORGOTTEN HIM! NO,
THIS WAS A NIGHT HE WOULD REMEMBER
FOR THE REST OF HIS LIFE BECAUSE BY
THIS TIME,

HE'D ONLY GOT HIS SOCKS ON!

NOTE: *when I compered an evening of popular classical music recently, I switched this joke and used it to introduce 'Il Seraglio' by Mozart. It is printed here in its newish form as an example of the way to switch a joke to tie in with a particular event.*

IF THEY LAUGH AT *THAT*,

GO TO ⟹ NEAREST ... EXIT.

OR PRETEND IT NEVER HAPPENED AND

GO BACK TO ⟹ E

OR CUT YOUR LOSSES AND

GO TO ⟹ F PERORATION

J9-1 *Switch*

IT WAS THE YEAR 1778, WHEN MOZART WAS A MEMBER OF THE ARCHBISHOP OF SALZBURG'S HOUSEHOLD. HE WENT INTO THE MORNING ROOM ONE MORNING, VERY DEPRESSED.

'ANYTHING WRONG, JOHANN?' SAID BRÜNHILDE VON PLINK, THE ARCH-BISHOP'S PRETTY YOUNG HOUSE-KEEPER.

'JA,' SAID MOZART. 'FIRSTLY, MY NAME IS *WOLFGANG*, AND SECONDLY THE ARCH-BISHOP HAS ORDERED ME TO LEAVE TO-MORROW BECAUSE I HAVE NOT WRITTEN HIM A NEW *OPERA*, AND NOBODY *CARES*! NO FAREWELL PARTY, NO GOLDEN HAND-PULL, NOTHING! SO MUCH FOR MY "FRIENDS"!

THE YOUNG HOUSE-KEEPER FLUTTERED HER LONG, PRE-SEXIST EYE-LASHES. 'WELL, WHY DON'T YOU HAVE A *PRIVATE* FAREWELL PARTY WITH *ME* ... TONIGHT ... WAS SAGST DU, MEIN LIEBER WOLFIE?'

WOLFGANG LOOKED AT HER, DRIBBLED A LITTLE WURST, AND SAID: 'MMMM? ACH ... JA. JA. JA. *JA!* BRÜNIE!'

95

'WELL, COME TO THE GRAND SUMMER-HOUSE ABOUT TEN O'CLOCK, GUT?'

HE WAS THERE AT NINE FIFTY-FIVE, IMMACULATELY DRESSED, SMOTHERED IN BRUT-CHEN, AND STUM AT THE SIGHT OF THE HOUSE-KEEPER IN A SILKEN BLOUSE AND CLINGING DIRNDL, LOOKING ABSO-LUTELY WUNDERLICH!

'EXCUSE ME, EINE KLEINE MOMENT,' SHE SAID, 'WHILE I SLIP INTO – THE OTHER ROOM!' MOZART STOOD THERE, WONDER-ING IF THIS FAREWELL PARTY WASN'T GOING TO BE THE BEST THING SINCE TERRY VON VOGAN, THEN SHE SAID THROUGH THE DOOR: 'NEARLY READY – JUST ANOTHER MOMENT – LIEBCHEN.'

THEN, AFTER A FEW MORE MINUTES, 'YOU CAN COME IN, NOW.'

HE OPENED THE DOOR – AND GAZED UPON THE MOST INCREDIBLE SIGHT HE HAD EVER SEEN! ALL HIS COLLEAGUES WERE THERE, HIS FELLOW MUSICIANS, HAYDN, GLÜCK, THE ARCHBISHOP OF SALZBURG AND HIS ENTIRE COURT, IN-CLUDING JIMMY VON SAVILLE UND PRIN-CESS MICHAEL VON KENT – SELLING BOOKS!

ALL WERE GATHERED ROUND A TABLE LOADED WITH KNACKWURST, SAUER-KRAUT, CHAMPAGNE, THE LOT! HIS FRIENDS HAD NOT FORGOTTEN HIM! NEIN! THIS WAS A NIGHT HE WOULD REMEMBER FOR THE REST OF HIS LIFE, BECAUSE BY THIS TIME *HE'D ONLY GOT HIS SOCKS ON!*

AND THAT'S WHY MOZART LEFT SALZ-BURG FOR VIENNA – AND WROTE 'IL SERAGLIO' (THE HAREM) K384, FROM WHICH YOU WILL NOW HEAR THE OVERTURE ...

NOTE ON $\boxed{\text{J10}}$: *this is an optional comic bit, which spins out the speech and warms up a broader kind of audience, straight after* $\boxed{\text{A}}$.

If you need still more spinning out, go on to $\boxed{\text{J11}}$.

J10 *Don't tell jokes*

IF YOU ARE REALLY STUCK, TELL THEM A JOKE! (To audience)
THAT'S A FAT LOT OF GOOD, I DON'T *TELL* JOKES. (Looking at these pages as if examining the material) AND CERTAINLY NOT *THIS* LOT! LOOK AT THEM! WHY, THESE DAYS THEY'RE ALL ABOUT PAKISTANIS AND POLES AND IRISHMEN, AND THAT IS DISGRACEFUL AND INEXCUSABLE *PRE-JUDICE*, AND I *REFUSE* TO TELL JOKES LIKE THAT, ABSOLUTELY *REFUSE* TO TELL ANY OF THAT *RACIST FILTH* – LIKE THE ONE ABOUT THE IRISHMAN WHO WAS ARREST-ED FOR RAPE SO THEY PUT HIM INTO AN IDENTIFICATION PARADE AND WHEN THEY BROUGHT IN THE GIRL WHO'D BEEN RAPED HE SAID: *'THAT'S THE ONE!'* I *REFUSE* TO TELL JOKES LIKE THAT! AND IF THEY'RE NOT ABOUT RACE, THEY'RE ABOUT *SEX*, *EQUALLY* DEGRADING AND MORALLY DESTRUCTIVE LIKE THE ONE ABOUT THE WOMAN WHO WAS GRANTED A DIVORCE WHEN SHE TOLD THE JUDGE HER HUSBAND SPOKE TO HER ONLY *THREE* TIMES IN THE COURSE OF THEIR MARRIAGE – SHE WAS GRANTED THE CUSTODY OF THE THREE CHILDREN.

YOU'LL *NEVER* HEAR *ME* TELL *THAT*!

THEN IF THEY'RE NOT ABOUT RACE OR SEX THEY'RE JUST PLAIN *STUPID*, AND IF I WERE TO TELL ONE OF THOSE, IT WOULD NOT BE VERY FLATTERING TO *YOU* – LIKE THE ONE ABOUT THE MAN WHO WENT TO HIS DOCTOR AND SAID: 'DOCTOR, EVERY-ONE *IGNORES* ME! WHEN I GO TO WORK, MY MATES SEND ME TO COVENTRY, WHEN I GO TO BED, MY WIFE TURNS HER BACK ON ME, AND THE DOCTOR SAID *'NEXT!'*

I WOULDN'T INSULT YOUR INTELLIGENCE WITH A JOKE LIKE *THAT* – I'D INSULT *YOU*, BUT NOT YOUR INTELLIGENCE.

GO TO ⟹ J11

IF NOTHING WORKS WITH THIS LOT,
GIVE THEM A SHORT BURST OF:

J11 *Max Miller*

J11-1

OH, I LIKE THE GIRLS THAT DO
AND I LIKE THE GIRLS THAT DON'T
AND I HATE THE ONE THAT SAYS SHE WILL
AND THEN SHE SAYS SHE WON'T!
BUT THE ONE I LIKE BEST OF ALL
AND I KNOW YOU'LL THINK I'M RIGHT
IS THE ONE THAT SAYS SHE NEVER HAS
BUT LOOKS AS IF SHE – NOW THERE'S
A FUNNY THING!

J11-2

A BOY AND A GIRL WENT OUT HIKING
OF COURSE, THEY WERE BOTH WEARING
    SHORTS;
THEY STOPPED AT THE OLD PIG AND
    WHISTLE
AND THERE HAD A COUPLE OF PORTS.
WHEN THEY GOT BACK IN THE EVENING,
THE NEIGHBOURS ALL STARTED TO QUIZ,
FOR HE CAME HOME LATE WEARING HER
    SHORTS –
SHE CAME HOME LATE WEARING HIS! OY!

J11-3

JACK AND JILL WENT UP THE HILL
JUST LIKE TWO COCK LINNETS
JILL CAME DOWN WITH HALF A CROWN
SHE WASN'T UP *THERE* TWO MINUTES –
    HERE!

IF THEY LAUGH AT *THIS*

GO TO ⟹ SEALED SECTION AT THE
BACK
OR
DON'T MIND IF THEY WALK OUT – IT'S
WHEN THEY START COMING TOWARDS
YOU, YOU SHOULD WORRY!

OR
GO TO ⟹ B WHY ARE WE HERE?
        C WHO'S HERE?

NOTE: *the 'Ad lib' or 'Heckler stopper' is the cabaret comedian's secret weapon. In rare cases where the audience is too lively it is good to have a riposte or two up your sleeve. But they are merely an insurance and no match for your native wit.*

J12 Ad libs

SHOULD YOU BE PLAGUED BY POINTLESS-
LY PERSISTENT IMPROMPTU REPARTEE,
MERELY SLING A FEW OF THESE DOWN:

J12-1 *Heckler stoppers*
● I GET PAID FOR ACTING STUPID –WHAT'S
YOUR EXCUSE?
● I HOPE I RUN INTO YOU *AGAIN* ONE DAY –
WHEN YOU'RE WALKING AND I'M DRIV-
ING.
● WHAT'S ALL THE COMMOTION? – NO
SCHOOL TOMORROW?

J12-2 *Groucho Marx*
● I NEVER FORGET A FACE, BUT IN *YOUR*
CASE, I'LL MAKE AN EXCEPTION.
● DIDN'T I MEET YOU IN MONTE CARLO
THE NIGHT YOU SHOT YOURSELF?
● I REFUSE TO JOIN ANY CLUB THAT
WOULD HAVE *ME* AS A MEMBER!'

J12-3 *Women*
AND IF THE WOMEN'S LIBBERS AD LIB:
● A WOMAN'S WORLD IS NEVER DONE.
● NOW I KNOW WHY ADAM WAS CREATED
FIRST – IT GAVE HIM A CHANCE TO SAY
SOMETHING.
● A WOMAN'S PLACE IS IN THE WRONG.

Appendix

NOTE: *this appendix contains a useful selection of half-heard, half-remembered quotations, some chunks of purple prose to spark up or send up your subject, and space to put in a few of your own favourites.*

Quotations

Q1 From Britain

Q1-1 'If' by Rudyard Kipling

IF YOU CAN KEEP YOUR HEAD WHEN ALL ABOUT YOU

ARE LOSING THEIRS AND BLAMING IT ON YOU,

IF YOU CAN TRUST YOURSELF WHEN ALL MEN DOUBT YOU,

BUT MAKE ALLOWANCE FOR THEIR DOUBTING TOO;

IF YOU CAN WAIT AND NOT BE TIRED BY WAITING,

OR BEING LIED ABOUT, DON'T DEAL IN LIES,

OR BEING HATED, DON'T GIVE WAY TO HATING,

AND YET DON'T LOOK TOO GOOD, NOR TALK TOO WISE:

IF YOU CAN DREAM – AND NOT MAKE DREAMS YOUR MASTER;

IF YOU CAN THINK – AND NOT MAKE THOUGHTS YOUR AIM;

IF YOU CAN MEET WITH TRIUMPH AND DISASTER

AND TREAT THOSE TWO IMPOSTERS JUST THE SAME.

IF YOU CAN MAKE ONE HEAP OF ALL YOUR WINNINGS

AND RISK IT ON ONE TURN OF PITCH-AND-TOSS,

AND LOSE, AND START AGAIN AT YOUR BEGINNINGS

AND NEVER BREATHE A WORD ABOUT YOUR LOSS.

IF YOU CAN TALK WITH CROWDS AND KEEP YOUR VIRTUE,

OR WALK WITH KINGS – NOR LOSE THE COMMON TOUCH,

IF NEITHER FOES NOR LOVING FRIENDS CAN HURT YOU,

Q1

Micawber
W.C.
FIELDS

IF ALL MEN COUNT WITH YOU, BUT NONE
 TOO MUCH,
IF YOU CAN FILL THE UNFORGIVING
 MINUTE
WITH SIXTY SECONDS WORTH OF
 DISTANCE RUN,
YOURS IS THE EARTH AND EVERYTHING
 THAT'S IN IT,
AND – WHICH IS MORE – YOU'LL BE A MAN,
 MY SON!

Q1-2 *Micawber's advice, from 'David Copperfield'*
AT PRESENT, AND UNTIL SOMETHING
TURNS UP (WHICH I AM, I MAY SAY,
HOURLY EXPECTING) I HAVE NOTHING TO
BESTOW BUT ADVICE. STILL MY ADVICE IS
SO FAR WORTH TAKING THAT – IN SHORT,
THAT I HAVE NEVER TAKEN IT MYSELF
AND AM THE MISERABLE WRETCH YOU
BEHOLD. MY ADVICE IS, NEVER DO
TOMORROW WHAT YOU CAN DO TODAY.
PROCRASTINATION IS THE THIEF OF TIME.
COLLAR HIM!... MY OTHER PIECE OF
ADVICE, COPPERFIELD... YOU KNOW.
ANNUAL INCOME TWENTY POUNDS,
ANNUAL EXPENDITURE NINETEEN NINE-
TEEN SIX, RESULT HAPPINESS. ANNUAL
INCOME TWENTY POUNDS, ANNUAL
EXPENDITURE TWENTY POUNDS OUGHT
AND SIX, RESULT MISERY. THE BLOSSOM IS
BLIGHTED, THE LEAF IS WITHERED, THE
GOD OF DAY GOES DOWN UPON THE
DREARY SCENE, AND – AND IN SHORT YOU
ARE FOR EVER FLOORED. AS I AM!'

Q1-3 *Disraeli on Gladstone*
AS BENJAMIN DISRAELI SAID OF WILLIAM
EWART GLADSTONE IN 1878; HE IS 'A
SOPHISTICATED RHETORICIAN, INEBRI-
ATED WITH THE EXUBERANCE OF HIS
OWN VERBOSITY, AND GIFTED WITH AN
EGOTISTICAL IMAGINATION, THAT CAN
AT ALL TIMES COMMAND AN INTERMIN-
ABLE AND INCONSISTENT SERIES OF
ARGUMENTS TO MALIGN HIS OPPONENTS,
AND GLORIFY HIMSELF.'

NOTE: *I can't resist (with this delicious whiff of nostalgia for a time when the map of the World was coloured with large areas of British Red) a modest demonstration of the way to switch a poem as well as a joke. First let them mock the old values, then sock it to them with the 'superiority' of their own.*

OR, MORE SUCCINCTLY: 'HE HAS NOT A SINGLE AND REDEEMING DEFECT.'

(TO WHICH YOU ADD: 'WHICH BRINGS ME TO OUR GUEST OF HONOUR...)

Q1-4 *Vitai lampada* by Sir Henry Newbolt

THERE'S A BREATHLESS HUSH IN THE CLOSE TONIGHT –
TEN TO MAKE AND THE MATCH TO WIN –
A BUMPING PITCH AND A BLINDING LIGHT,
AN HOUR TO PLAY AND THE LAST MAN IN.
AND IT'S NOT FOR THE SAKE OF A RIBBONED COAT,
OR THE SELFISH HOPE OF A SEASON'S FAME,
BUT HIS CAPTAIN'S HAND ON HIS SHOULDER SMOTE –
'PLAY UP! PLAY UP! AND PLAY THE GAME!'

IF YOU WERE TO RECITE THOSE WORDS TODAY BEFORE A GATHERING OF MODERN BRITISH YOUTH – AT A POP CONCERT, FOR EXAMPLE, SANDWICHED BETWEEN ROD STEWART, THAT FRESH-FACED LYRIC TENOR, AND A GROUP OF PUNK ROCKERS, THOSE MASTERS OF THE ENGLISH LANGUAGE – THEY WOULD THINK YOU HAD GONE RIGHT OUT OF YOUR TINY MIND! TO APPEAL TO THE *MODERN* CHILD, YOU WOULD NEED A SLIGHT SHIFT OF EMPHASIS:

THERE'S AN UGLY ROAR AT THE MATCH TODAY –
IT'S A GOAL! AND THE WRONG SIDE'S WON –
THERE'S MORE THAN ONE SCORE TO BE SETTLED HERE,
BEFORE THIS 'SPORTING' DAY IS DONE!
THE RIVER OF HATE HAS BRIMMED HIS BANKS,
THERE'S A SPLASH OF BLOOD ON A DENIM SUIT,
AS THE VOICE OF A SCHOOLBOY RALLIES THE RANKS –
'THE BOOT! THE BOOT! PUT IN THE BOOT!'

WINSTON SPENCER CHURCHILL

Punch, 1893

NEARLY ALL OUR BEST MEN ARE DEAD!
CARLYLE, TENNYSON, BROWNING,
  GEORGE ELIOT.
I'M NOT FEELING VERY WELL MYSELF.

NOTE: *a modern switch?*
NEARLY ALL THE BEST COMEDIANS ARE
DEAD! GROUCHO MARX, BUSTER KEATON,
JACK BENNY, SARAH BERNHARDT! I'M
NOT FEELING SO GOOD MYSELF.

Q1-6 *Sir Winston Leonard Spencer Churchill*
House of Commons, June 4th 1940
WE SHALL NOT FLAG OR FAIL. WE SHALL
FIGHT IN FRANCE, WE SHALL FIGHT ON
THE SEAS AND OCEANS, WE SHALL FIGHT
WITH GROWING CONFIDENCE AND
GROWING STRENGTH IN THE AIR, WE
SHALL DEFEND OUR ISLAND, WHATEVER
THE COST MAY BE, WE SHALL FIGHT ON
THE BEACHES, WE SHALL FIGHT ON THE
LANDING GROUNDS, WE SHALL FIGHT IN
THE FIELDS AND IN THE STREETS, WE
SHALL FIGHT IN THE HILLS; WE SHALL
NEVER SURRENDER.

House of Commons, June 18th 1940

LET US THEREFORE BRACE OURSELVES
TO OUR DUTY AND SO BEAR OURSELVES
THAT IF THE BRITISH COMMONWEALTH
AND EMPIRE LASTS FOR A THOUSAND
YEARS MEN WILL STILL SAY, 'THIS WAS
THEIR FINEST HOUR.'

House of Commons, August 20th 1940

NEVER IN THE FIELD OF HUMAN CON-
FLICT WAS SO MUCH OWED BY SO MANY
TO SO FEW.

'A sonnet from the Portuguese'
by Elizabeth Barrett Browning

HOW DO I LOVE THEE? LET ME COUNT THE
    WAYS.
I LOVE THEE TO THE DEPTH AND BREADTH
    AND HEIGHT
MY SOUL CAN REACH, WHEN FEELING OUT
    OF SIGHT
FOR THE ENDS OF BEING AND IDEAL
    GRACE.
I LOVE THEE TO THE LEVEL OF EVERY
    DAY'S
MOST QUIET NEED, BY SUN AND CANDLE-
    LIGHT.
I LOVE THEE FREELY, AS MEN STRIVE FOR
    RIGHT.
I LOVE THEE PURELY, AS MEN TURN FROM
    PRAISE.
I LOVE THEE WITH THE PASSION PUT TO
    USE
IN MY OLD GRIEFS, AND WITH MY CHILD-
    HOOD'S FAITH.
I LOVE THEE WITH A LOVE I SEEMED TO
    LOSE
WITH MY LOST SAINTS – I LOVE THEE
    WITH THE BREATH,
SMILES, TEARS, OF ALL MY LIFE! – AND, IF
    GOD CHOOSE,
I SHALL BUT LOVE THEE BETTER AFTER
    DEATH.

Q1-8 Virginia Woolf (1882–1941)
WOMEN HAVE SERVED ALL THESE CEN-
TURIES AS LOOKING-GLASSES POSSESSING
THE MAGIC AND DELICIOUS POWER OF
REFLECTING THE FIGURE OF MAN AT
TWICE ITS NATURAL SIZE.

Q2 *From America*

Q2-1 *Mark Twain (Samuel Clemens, 1835–1910)*

AS MARK TWAIN MIGHT HAVE PUT IT AND DID: I AM DIFFERENT FROM WASHINGTON. I HAVE A HIGHER AND GRANDER STANDARD OF PRINCIPLE. WASHINGTON COULD *NOT LIE*! I *CAN* LIE, BUT I *WON'T*!

I DON'T MIND WHAT THE OPPOSITION *SAY* OF ME, SO LONG AS THEY DON'T TELL THE *TRUTH* ABOUT ME – BUT WHEN THEY *DESCEND* TO TELLING THE *TRUTH* ABOUT ME, I CONSIDER THAT THAT IS TAKING AN *UNFAIR* ADVANTAGE!

IF YOU PICK UP A STARVING DOG AND MAKE HIM PROSPEROUS, HE WILL NOT BITE YOU.
THIS IS THE PRINCIPAL DIFFERENCE BETWEEN A DOG AND A MAN.

Q2-2 *Thomas Wolfe (1900–38)*

IF A MAN HAS A TALENT AND CANNOT USE IT, HE HAS FAILED. IF HE HAS A TALENT AND USES ONLY HALF OF IT, HE HAS PARTLY FAILED. IF HE HAS A TALENT AND LEARNS SOMEHOW TO USE THE WHOLE OF IT, HE HAS GLORIOUSLY SUCCEEDED, AND WON A SATISFACTION AND A TRIUMPH FEW MEN EVER KNOW.

Man's comment: 'MORE, MORE! WE NEED IT!'

Q2-3 *American Declaration of Independence (Thomas Jefferson), July 4th 1776*

WE HOLD THESE TRUTHS TO BE SELF-EVIDENT, THAT ALL MEN ARE CREATED EQUAL, THAT THEY ARE ENDOWED BY THEIR CREATOR WITH CERTAIN UN-ALIENABLE RIGHTS, THAT AMONG THESE ARE LIFE, LIBERTY, AND THE PURSUIT OF HAPPINESS.

Q2

Q2-4 *Abraham Lincoln. Gettysburg address,*
November 19th 1863

FOURSCORE AND SEVEN YEARS AGO OUR
FATHERS BROUGHT FORTH UPON THIS
CONTINENT A NEW NATION, CONCEIVED
IN LIBERTY, AND DEDICATED TO THE PRO-
POSITION THAT ALL MEN ARE CREATED
EQUAL. NOW WE ARE ENGAGED IN A
GREAT CIVIL WAR, TESTING WHETHER
THAT NATION, OR ANY NATION SO CON-
CEIVED AND SO DEDICATED, CAN LONG
ENDURE. WE ARE MET ON A GREAT
BATTLEFIELD OF THAT WAR. WE HAVE
COME TO DEDICATE A PORTION OF THAT
FIELD AS A FINAL RESTING-PLACE OF
THOSE WHO HERE GAVE THEIR LIVES
THAT THAT NATION MIGHT LIVE. IT IS
ALTOGETHER FITTING AND PROPER THAT
WE SHOULD DO THIS. BUT IN A LARGER
SENSE WE CANNOT DEDICATE, WE CAN-
NOT CONSECRATE, WE CANNOT HALLOW
THIS GROUND. THE BRAVE MEN, LIVING
AND DEAD, WHO STRUGGLED HERE, HAVE
CONSECRATED IT FAR ABOVE OUR POWER
TO ADD OR DETRACT. THE WORLD WILL
LITTLE NOTE, NOR LONG REMEMBER,
WHAT WE SAY HERE, BUT IT CAN NEVER
FORGET WHAT THEY DID HERE. IT IS FOR
US, THE LIVING, RATHER TO BE DEDI-
CATED HERE TO THE UNFINISHED WORK
THEY HAVE THUS FAR SO NOBLY AD-
VANCED. IT IS RATHER FOR US TO BE HERE
DEDICATED TO THE GREAT TASK REMAIN-
ING BEFORE US, THAT FROM THESE
HONOURED DEAD WE TAKE INCREASED
DEVOTION TO THAT CAUSE FOR WHICH
THEY HERE GAVE THE LAST FULL MEASURE
OF DEVOTION; THAT WE HERE HIGHLY
RESOLVE THAT THE DEAD SHALL NOT
HAVE DIED IN VAIN, THAT THIS NATION,
UNDER GOD, SHALL HAVE A NEW BIRTH
OF FREEDOM; AND THAT GOVERNMENT OF
THE PEOPLE, BY THE PEOPLE, AND FOR
THE PEOPLE, SHALL NOT PERISH FROM
THE EARTH.

NOTE: *how about this brought up to date:*

AND THIS IS GOOD OLD LONDON
THE HOME OF THE CHIP AND THE COD,
WHERE THE TEBBITS TALK TO THE
   THATCHERS
AND THE THATCHERS TALK ONLY TO GOD.

Q2-5 *Franklin Delano Roosevelt (1882–1945)*

IN THE FUTURE DAYS, WHICH WE SEEK TO MAKE SECURE, WE LOOK FORWARD TO A WORLD FOUNDED UPON FOUR ESSENTIAL FREEDOMS. THE FIRST IS FREEDOM OF SPEECH AND EXPRESSION – EVERYWHERE IN THE WORLD. THE SECOND IS FREEDOM OF EVERY PERSON TO WORSHIP GOD IN HIS OWN WAY, EVERYWHERE IN THE WORLD. THE THIRD IS FREEDOM FROM WANT... EVERYWHERE IN THE WORLD. THE FOURTH IS FREEDOM FROM FEAR... ANYWHERE IN THE WORLD.

Q2-3 *John Collins Bossidy (1860–1928)*

AND THIS IS GOOD OLD BOSTON,
THE HOME OF THE BEAN AND THE COD,
WHERE THE LOWELLS TALK TO THE CABOTS,
AND THE CABOTS TALK ONLY TO GOD.

Q2-7 *'Liquor and longevity' (anon)*

THE HORSE AND THE MULE LIVE 30 YEARS
AND NOTHING KNOW OF WINES AND BEERS.
THE GOAT AND SHEEP AT 20 DIE
AND NEVER TASTE OF SCOTCH OR RYE.
THE COW DRINKS WATER BY THE TON
AND AT 18 IS MOSTLY DONE
THE DOG AT 15 CASHES IN
WITHOUT THE AID OF RUM AND GIN.
THE CAT IN MILK AND WATER SOAKS
AND THEN IN 12 SHORT YEARS IT CROAKS.
THE MODEST, SOBER, BONE-DRY HEN
LAYS EGGS FOR NOGS, THEN DIES AT TEN.
ALL ANIMALS ARE STRICTLY DRY;
THEY SINLESS LIVE AND SWIFTLY DIE;
BUT SINFUL, GINFUL RUM-SOAKED MEN
SURVIVE FOR THREE SCORE YEARS AND TEN.
AND SOME OF THEM, A VERY FEW,
STAY PICKLED TILL THEY'RE 92.

NOTE: *we all have our editions of the Bard, we all know bits of the soliloquies, but it is useful to pluck a few out and print them here. Quote them, mis-quote them, parody them, do what you like with them, they are just about out of copyright.*

Q3-1 *'Hamlet', Act 3 Scene 1*

TO BE, OR NOT TO BE, THAT IS THE QUESTION:

WHETHER 'TIS NOBLER IN THE MIND TO SUFFER

THE SLINGS AND ARROWS OF OUTRAGEOUS FORTUNE,

OF TO TAKE ARMS AGAINST A SEA OF TROUBLES,

AND BY OPPOSING, END THEM. TO DIE, TO SLEEP –

NO MORE, AND BY A SLEEP TO SAY WE END

THE HEART-ACHE AND THE THOUSAND NATURAL SHOCKS

THAT FLESH IS HEIR TO: 'TIS A CONSUMMATION

DEVOUTLY TO BE WISH'D. TO DIE, TO SLEEP –

TO SLEEP PERCHANCE TO DREAM – AY, THERE'S THE RUB,

FOR IN THAT SLEEP OF DEATH WHAT DREAMS MAY COME

WHEN WE HAVE SHUFFLED OFF THIS MORTAL COIL,

MUST GIVE US PAUSE: THERE'S THE RESPECT

THAT MAKES CALAMITY OF SO LONG LIFE:

FOR WHO WOULD BEAR THE WHIPS AND SCORNS OF TIME,

THE OPPRESSOR'S WRONG, THE PROUD MAN'S CONTUMELY,

THE PANGS OF DISPRIZ'D LOVE, THE LAW'S DELAY

THE INSOLENCE OF OFFICE, AND THE SPURNS

THAT PATIENT MERIT OF THE UNWORTHY TAKES,

WHEN HE HIMSELF MIGHT HIS QUIETUS MAKE

WITH A BARE BODKIN; WHO WOULD FARDELS BEAR,

TO GRUNT AND SWEAT UNDER A WEARY LIFE,

BUT THAT THE DREAD OF SOMETHING AFTER DEATH,

THE UNDISCOVER'D COUNTRY FROM WHOSE BOURN

NO TRAVELLER RETURNS, PUZZLES THE WILL,

I LIKE BEING A KING

Richard III
OLIVIER

AND MAKES US RATHER BEAR THOSE ILLS
  WE HAVE,
THAN FLY TO OTHERS THAT WE KNOW
  NOT OF?
THUS CONSCIENCE DOTH MAKE COWARDS
  OF US ALL
AND THUS THE NATIVE HUE OF RESO-
  LUTION
IS SICKLED O'ER WITH THE PALE CAST OF
  THOUGHT,
AND ENTERPRISES OF GREAT PITH AND
  MOMENT
WITH THIS REGARD THEIR CURRENTS
  TURN AWRY,
AND LOSE THE NAME OF ACTION.

Q3-2 *'Richard III', Act 1 Scene 1*
NOW IS THE WINTER OF OUR DISCONTENT
MADE GLORIOUS SUMMER BY THIS SON OF
  YORK;
AND ALL THE CLOUDS THAT LOW'R'D
  UPON OUR HOUSE
IN THE DEEP BOSOM OF THE OCEAN
  BURIED.
NOW ARE OUR BROWS BOUND WITH
  VICTORIOUS WREATHS,
OUR BRUISED ARMS HUNG UP FOR MONU-
  MENTS,
OUR STERN ALARUMS CHANG'D TO MERRY
  MEETINGS,
OUR DREADFUL MARCHES TO DELIGHTFUL
  MEASURES.
GRIM-VISAG'D WAR HATH SMOOTH'D HIS
  WRINKLED FRONT;
AND NOW, INSTEAD OF MOUNTING BARBED
  STEEDS
TO FRIGHT THE SOULS OF FEARFUL
  ADVERSARIES,
HE CAPERS NIMBLY IN A LADY'S CHAMBER
TO THE LASCIVIOUS PLEASING OF A LUTE.
BUT I, THAT AM NOT SHAPED FOR SPORT-
  IVE TRICKS,
NOR MADE TO COURT AN AMOROUS
  LOOKING-GLASS;
I, THAT AM RUDELY STAMPED, AND WANT
  LOVE'S MAJESTY
TO STRUT BEFORE A WANTON AMBLING
  NYMPH;

NOTE: *when I presented the Variety Club Tribute to Sir Harry Secombe, I opened with this parody of the Prologue:*

O FOR A MUSE OF FUN THAT WOULD
    ASCEND
THE BRIGHTEST 'HIGHWAY' OF INVEN-
    TION!
THE GROSVENOR FOR A STAGE, CLOWN
    PRINCES TO ACT,
AND BARKERS TO BEHOLD THE SWAYING
    SCENE! HIC!
THEN SHOULD THE SUAVE SIR HARRY BE
    HIMSELF,
ASSUME THE AIR OF PUCK (I COME OUT IN A'
COLD SWEAT EVERY TIME I SAY THAT
LINE)
    ... AND AT HIS HEELS
(LEASH'D IN LIKE HOUNDS) SHOULD
    WHEEZES, SONGS AND WHOOPEE-
    CUSHIONS
CROUCH FOR EMPLOYMENT. BUT PARDON,
GENTILES ALL – ER – GENTLES ALL,

I, THAT AM CURTAIL'D OF THIS FAIR
  PROPORTION,
CHEATED OF FEATURE BY DISSEMBLING
  NATURE,
DEFORM'D, UNFINISH'D, SENT BEFORE MY
  TIME
INTO THIS BREATHING WORLD, SCARCE
  HALF MADE UP,
AND THAT SO LAMELY AND UNFASHION-
  ABLE
THAT DOGS BARK AT ME AS I HALT BY
  THEM –
WHY, I, IN THIS WEAK PIPING TIME OF
  PEACE,
HAVE NO DELIGHT TO PASS AWAY THE
  TIME,
UNLESS TO SEE MY SHADOW IN THE SUN
AND DESCANT ON MINE OWN DEFORMITY.
AND THEREFORE, SINCE I CANNOT PROVE
  A LOVER
TO ENTERTAIN THESE FAIR, WELL-SPOKEN
  DAYS,
I AM DETERMINED TO PROVE A VILLAIN
AND HATE THE IDLE PLEASURES OF THESE
  DAYS...

Q3-3 *'Henry V', Chorus, I*
O, FOR THE MUSE OF FIRE, THAT WOULD
  ASCEND
THE BRIGHTEST HEAVEN OF INVENTION!

A KINGDOM FOR A STAGE, PRINCES TO ACT,

AND MONARCHS TO BEHOLD THE SWELL-
  ING SCENE!
THEN SHOULD THE WAR-LIKE HARRY,
  LIKE HIMSELF,
ASSUME THE PORT OF MARS...

 ... AND AT HIS HEELS
(LEASH'D IN LIKE HOUNDS) SHOULD
  FAMINE, SWORD, AND FIRE

CROUCH FOR EMPLOYMENT, BUT PARDON,
  GENTLES ALL,

THE FLAT UNRAISED SPIRITS THAT HATH
  DAR'D
ON THIS UNWORTHY SCAFFOLD TO O.B. . . .
(OR NOT O.B. – THAT IS THE BUDGET –)
SO GREAT AN OBJECT. CAN THIS COCKPIT
  HOLD
THE VASTY HILLS OF NEDDY SEAGOON?
  OR MAY WE CRAM
WITHIN THIS WOODEN O HIS VERY GAGS

THAT DID AFRIGHT THE EAR AT SWANSEA
  EMPIRE?

NOTE: *to round off the parody, I moved to Act III, Scene
1, to introduce the Beverly Sisters.*

BUT SOFT, THERE IN THE WINGS
THREE HEAV'N-KISS'D MAIDENS
CURV'D LIKE BEVERLY'S HILLS
SEE HOW THEY STAND LIKE GREYHOUNDS
  IN THEIR SLIPS (AND BRAS)
STRAINING UPON THE START. THE GAME'S
  AFOOT!
COME, TUNESOME THREESOME AND UPON
  THIS STAGE
CRY, 'GOD FOR HARRY, SECOMBE, AND
  THE BEVS!'

THE FLAT UNRAISED SPIRITS THAT HATH
     DAR'D
ON THIS UNWORTHY SCAFFOLD TO BRING
     FORTH
SO GREAT AN OBJECT. CAN THIS COCKPIT
     HOLD
THE VASTY FIELDS OF FRANCE? OR MAY
     WE CRAM
WITHIN THIS WOODEN O THE VERY
     CASQUES
THAT DID AFFRIGHT THE EAR AT AGIN-
     COURT?

Act 3, Scene 1

I SEE YOU STAND LIKE GREYHOUNDS IN
     THE SLIPS,
STRAINING UPON THE START. THE GAME'S
     A FOOT!
FOLLOW YOUR SPIRIT, AND UPON THIS
     CHARGE
CRY, 'GOD FOR HARRY, ENGLAND, AND
     SAINT GEORGE!'

NOTE: *when addressing a charity audience (and developing your appeal in section* $\boxed{E}$ *) it adds a lighter touch if you read out the comments* (RED CAPITALS) *after each degree of charity.*

NOTE: *here's one way to relate the 'eight degrees' of Maimonides to your fund-raising occasion.*

Q4-1 *Maimonides (1135-1204) on charity*

ACCORDING TO MAIMONIDES, THERE ARE *EIGHT ASCENDING DEGREES* IN THE GIVING OF CHARITY:

1. HE WHO GIVES *GRUDGINGLY*.
(AS TO THE INLAND REVENUE)

2. HE WHO GIVES *GRACIOUSLY* – BUT *LESS* THAN HE SHOULD.
(AS WHEN TIPPING A TAXI DRIVER)

3. HE WHO GIVES GRACIOUSLY WHAT HE SHOULD BUT ONLY *AFTER HE IS ASKED*.
(OTHERWISE KNOWN AS 'I GAVE AT THE OFFICE')

4. HE WHO GIVES GRACIOUSLY *BEFORE* HE IS ASKED.
(SO HOW DOES HE KNOW WHO NEEDS IT?)

5. HE WHO GIVES *PUBLICLY* WITHOUT KNOWING TO WHOM HE GIVES.
(WHICH IS WHAT MOST OF US DO)

6. HE WHO GIVES *ANONYMOUSLY*.
(BUT YOU HAVE TO TELL THEM WHO IT'S FROM OR THEY DON'T KNOW WHO'S BEING ANONYMOUS)

7. HE WHO GIVES ANONYMOUSLY, WITH-OUT KNOWING TO WHOM HE GIVES.
(AS WHEN LEAVING THE SAFE OPEN FOR BURGLARS)

8. HE WHO BY A *GIFT* OR *LOAN* OR FINDING *EMPLOYMENT*, HELPS A FELLOW MAN TO *SUPPORT HIMSELF*.
(WHICH BRINGS US BACK TO THE INLAND REVENUE)

WELL, TODAY, IT THINK WE MAY SAFELY SAY THAT IT DOESN'T MATTER IF YOU GIVE GRUDGINGLY, OR LESS THAT YOU SHOULD, OR ONLY AFTER YOU ARE ASKED AND THEN SHOUT IT FROM THE ROOFTOPS *WE'LL TAKE IT ANYWAY YOU LIKE!* –

Q4

Nearham Rotary Club

WHAT *DOES* MATTER IS THAT YOU ARE HELPING YOUR FELLOW MEN TO SUPPORT THEMSELVES THROUGH A MAGNIFICENT INSTITUTION ....

....

AND THERE'S ONLY ONE WORD FOR THAT – ON A SCALE OF EIGHT, YOU'RE *TEN!*

Q4-2 *The Bible. Ruth 1: 16*
INTREAT ME NOT TO LEAVE THEE, OR TO RETURN FROM FOLLOWING AFTER THEE: FOR WHITHER THOU GOEST, I WILL GO: AND WHERE THOU LODGEST, I WILL LODGE: THY PEOPLE SHALL BE MY PEOPLE, AND THY GOD MY GOD.

Q4-3 *The Bible. Ecclesiastes 1: 2*
VANITY OF VANITIES, SAITH THE PREACHER, VANITY OF VANITIES; ALL IS VANITY.

Q4-4 *The Bible. Matthew 5: 3-10: the Sermon on the Mount.*
BLESSED ARE THE POOR IN SPIRIT: FOR THEIRS IS THE KINGDOM OF HEAVEN.
BLESSED ARE THEY THAT MOURN: FOR THEY SHALL BE COMFORTED.
BLESSED ARE THE MEEK: FOR THEY SHALL INHERIT THE EARTH.
BLESSED ARE THEY WHICH DO HUNGER AND THIRST AFTER RIGHTEOUSNESS: FOR THEY SHALL BE FILLED.
BLESSED ARE THE MERCIFUL: FOR THEY SHALL OBTAIN MERCY.
BLESSED ARE THE PURE IN HEART: FOR THEY SHALL SEE GOD.
BLESSED ARE THE PEACEMAKERS: FOR THEY SHALL BE CALLED THE CHILDREN OF GOD.
BLESSED ARE THEY WHICH ARE PERSECUTED FOR RIGHTEOUSNESS' SAKE: FOR THEIRS IS THE KINGDOM OF HEAVEN.

Today I am a Fountain Pen!

WOODY ALLEN

BY JEWISH TRADITION, 13 IS A *LUCKY* NUMBER. IT IS THE AGE WHEN A BOY IS BARMITZVAHED, THAT IS, WHEN HE BECOMES A MAN IN HIS COMMUNITY AND TAKES ON ALL THE RESPONSIBILITIES OF *MANHOOD* – MARRIAGE, MORTGAGES, INCOME TAX AND VAT! A *VERY* LUCKY NUMBER!

UP TO THE AGE OF 13, IF A BOY OPENS HIS MOUTH IN TEMPLE, HE GETS A CLIP ROUND THE EAR. AFTER 13, IT HURTS MORE AND IT'S CALLED A *DONATION*.

THESE DAYS THEY SPEND MORE MONEY ON BARMITZVAHS THAN THEY DO ON WEDDINGS: THEY KNOW WHICH IS GOING TO *LAST*.

John Smith

Q5 *Graffiti*

.... 'S WITTICISMS
ARE READ BY MORE PEOPLE THAN THOSE
OF ANY OTHER WRITER IN ENGLAND – IF
YOU DON'T BELIEVE ME, JUST LOOK ON
THE WALL OF THE MEN'S ROOM IN EUSTON
STATION!

HERE ARE SOME OF HIS MOST FAMOUS
APHORISMS:

IS KARL MARX'S GRAVE JUST A COMMUN-
IST PLOT?

I *LOVE* MANKIND! IT'S *PEOPLE* I CAN'T
STAND!

WOMEN SHOULDN'T WORRY ABOUT THE
MEN-O-PAUSE – THEY SHOULD WORRY
ABOUT THE MEN WHO DON'T!

TIRED OF SIN? IF NOT RING . . .

JESUS SAVES! WITH THE ABBEY NATIONAL.

GET THE ABBEY HABIT – SLEEP WITH A
MONK.

CHURCH PARKING ONLY. OFFENDERS
WILL BE BAPTISED.

TEMPLE PARKING ONLY. OFFENDERS WILL
BE CIRCUMCISED.

APPENDIX $\boxed{T}$

Toasts

T1 | Irish toasts

T1-1

MAY THE ROAD RISE UP TO MEET YOU
MAY THE WIND BE ALWAYS AT YOUR BACK
THE SUN SHINE WARM UPON YOUR FACE
THE RAIN FALL SOFT UPON YOUR FIELDS
AND UNTIL WE MEET AGAIN
MAY GOD HOLD YOU IN THE PALM OF HIS
  HAND.

T1-2

HEALTH AND LONG LIFE TO YOU
THE WIFE OF YOUR CHOICE TO YOU
A CHILD EVERY YEAR TO YOU
LAND WITHOUT RENT TO YOU
AND MAY YOU BE IN HEAVEN HALF AN
  HOUR
BEFORE THE DEVIL KNOWS YOU'RE DEAD.

T1-3

MAY YOUR MILK NEVER TURN
MAY YOUR HORSES NEVER STRAY
MAY YOUR HENS ALWAYS LAY
MAY THE MOON BE AS FULL AS YOUR GLASS
AND AMERICAN DOLLARS ARRIVE IN THE
  POST BY XMAS!
AND I HOPE, BEFORE YOU'RE MUCH OLDER
THAT YOU'LL HEAR BETTER TOASTS THAN
  THIS! SLAINTE!

T1-4

MAY THE HORNS OF YOUR CATTLE TOUCH
  HEAVEN
MAY THE ROCKS IN YOUR FIELD TURN TO
  GOLD
MAY THE THATCH ON YOUR HOUSE BE AS
  STRONG AS THE THATCH ON YOUR HEAD
MAY WHAT GOES DOWN TODAY NOT
  COME BACK UP AGAIN
AND MAY YOU DIE IN BED AT NINETY-FIVE
  YEARS SHOT BY A JEALOUS HUSBAND.

T1

John Smith

T2 *Other toasts*

T2-1

HERE'S A HEALTH TO YOU AND YOURS
WHO HAVE DONE SUCH THINGS FOR US
AND OURS; AND WHEN WE AND OURS
HAVE IT IN OUR POWERS TO DO FOR YOU
AND YOURS WHAT YOU AND YOURS HAVE
DONE FOR US AND OURS, THEN WE AND
OURS WILL DO FOR YOU AND YOURS
WHAT YOU AND YOURS HAVE DONE FOR
OURS. ALL TOGETHER NOW!

T2-2

HERE'S TO THE GIRL WHO LIVES ON THE
    HILL
SHE SAYS SHE WON'T BUT HER SISTER
    WILL
SO HERE'S TO HER SISTER!

T2-3

HERE'S TO EVE, GRANDAM OF OUR RACE
WHO WORE A FIG LEAF IN JUST THE RIGHT
    PLACE
AND HERE'S TO ADAM, GRANDAD OF US
    ALL
WHO WAS RIGHT ON THE SPOT
WHEN SHE LET THE LEAF FALL.

IF THEY LAUGH AT T2-2 AND T2-3

GO TO ⟩ J11 (MAX MILLER)

T2-4

HERE'S TO ....
MAY HE LIVE TO BE AS OLD AS HIS JOKES.

T2-5

HERE'S TO ALL OF US!
FOR THERE'S SO MUCH GOOD IN THE
    WORST OF US
AND SO MUCH BAD IN THE BEST OF US,
THAT IT HARDLY BEHOOVES ANY OF US
TO TALK ABOUT THE REST OF US.

AND A TOAST TO THE:
ARABS: BISMILLAH!
CHINESE: YUM SEN!
DANISH: SKAL!
FRENCH: SANTÉ!
GERMAN: PROSIT!
GREEK: EIS IGIAN!
ITALIAN: SALUTE
DANISH: SKÅL!
FRENCH: SANTÉ!
GERMANS: PROSIT!
GREEKS: EIS IGIAN!
ITALIANS: SALUTE!
JAPANESE: BANZAI!
JEWS: L'CHAIM!
RUSSIANS:
   NA ZDOROVIA!
SPANISH: SALUD!
WELSH: LECHYD DA!
IRISH: SLAINTE WAH!
ZULUS: OOGY WAWA!